The War
Against Society

A True Story...

A book by Author Jesper Persson

From Smith to criminal and the way back.
(Only in Sweden)

Big thanks to!
The following people have been very supportive to me during the writing.

Thanks to you! So I could write down my gloomy life story!

Chairman of the federation Christer. K
Governing committee Lasse. L
Author Michael. L
Individual Ingela. L
Individual Mossan
Individual Lollo

But the biggest thanks, of course, I give my children
Tobias and Alexander ho still call me dad!
Daddy loves you!
I will also give Anna one big thanks, because you raised the boys when I asked for it.
Anna I also want to say sorry for all the stupid things i`ve done over the years, where you and oure children have suffered.

Love Jesper

I give you mine lifestory, one lifestory you never forgot. I are not proud over my life or this crime I did. But I are proud over my kids and at I could tell you all my story on paper.

To you which is a sensitive person I already want too warn too much nasty and scary events in this book.

Much pleasure

Prologue

Many write books to earn their living, and have it as their regular source of income, which is normal procedur. Personaly, I have written this book for two diffrent reasons.

Want through this book to provide quite ordinary people, an explanation how easy things go wrong, and how difficult that is to stop it.
This book explaining how major shortcomings that are is our right society, and, as with these shortcommings is actually a major contributing factor, that many people fall outside the system.

Society is based on great chart for politican, who knows the truth, but hiding behind statisticans, which now show that crime rates fall in live their vulnerable goals. Truth knows most about, and has certainly already established political curtain, as a playful only politicans have to drench their own bad conscience.

The second part of this book, describes my own commitments as a criminal, total whitout conscience and empathy for other people. By reading this book, you will see how man ascends more and more out of society, in slow but brutal way, both mentally and physically. And the strange thing about it is, that you as a person do not realize it yourself until you stand there as the worst bus and hated by society.

That I made life sick for many people is something I have to live with the rest of my life, and they are exposed with their misery. To say that everything should be done would be just a big lie. You can only try to explain what happened and why. Probably a bad comfort for an exposed person, but maybe a help to understand it better, than to think it was personal.

Many will surely their conscience by signing, its a goal I personally do not have but just want to say it with my own words. What other people will like about me, is up to them. I dont want to influence their attitude about what they thinking about me.

So if you are a Smith or an exposed person you will regardless of profile, get a new view of this legal community. You will read by these lines, how I as a person changed from an ordinary person with houses, children, dogs, and to be a criminal empathetic soul.

Chapter 1

I was born and raised in Kingdom of Sweden, in Skåne county.

Already like a little powerful child I got a special upbringing, my parents worked in my grandfathers business which was carried out with sheetmetal, I became more or less grown up in the workshop, or home with my grandmother who grew up to me for the most part, with good results. My grandmother has always meant incredibly much, for both me and my upbringing. Its was she who had to become the parents figure thats my mother and father would have been in normal cases.

My grandmother never hesitated when it came to me, and always on hand as a safe backing for me. The biggest part of my growing up was with my grandmother.
My grandmother and grandfather ran a business, and so did I offen bring them to the workshop, which was a highlight to be on. There were giant machines used in this profession. I remember one maskin, how you call edge equipment, and used when cracking or bending sheet pieces.
A maskin that was incredibly tall and big in my little world. That was also this maskin ho my grandfather banned me to touch, then there was a high risk of clamping wiith my little hands. When my grandfather tells something, you never forgot it. My grandfather had extremely big eyebrows, that he pulled together when he was on a more determind mood. He was a very kind, but determind person you would not be angry with.

He had the ability just look at me, and I know to

sharpened or would his determind eyebrows collapse in the nasty way you would not ask for.

Then I was home with my grandparents in theres home, I had a par of ornamentslippers, as my grandmother had hung up on the wall inside the frontdoor, this slippers I have a clear memory of.

I had always this slippers when I ran around on grandmas lawn and played football. I have a strong memory of them, because I always fell when I had them on me.

As clear as I remember, my grandmother came running every time I fall, and that helped me back up. That I ran and fall all the way around, probably due to the fact that I was a round little guy, with a few extra kilos too much. And with a blue seamstress, and splendid as Thore Skogman as well as a side leg that was not to play with. Stupid times I hit myself and got sad, always my grandmother comforted with, Its over when you marry! I was at my grandparents at last from 6 years old to 12 years age. I do not know which one feels most annoying, At my parents not took me home or that, I have no memory of my mother doing any activites with me.
 Frankly,
I can not get on anything my mother did. As example, an outing or played game. It does not matters now, but the question is about my parents passive presence has created a greater need for me to be seen.

One question I wonder about today?

There was one activites my mother do, and that was to go to the emergencyroom in the middle of the night, in the smallest case. I dont now how many nigths I have sitting on an emergency room, beacuse of her infected condition of illness.

But I had give my father a little praise, when he went to the tivoli, circus and a number of trips to Denmark with me. Now Im not convinced that Denmarks trips were for my sake. Perhaps beacuse the beer had ended at home.
 I dont now? With my hand in hand, I can not say we did so much together.

But my father had not so easy at home when he was kid. Nothing I researched Its more a feeling. He was born during the war years and it was not that easy at the time. When you writting your own book, then you get a lot to think about.
I can not praise my parents, they certainly did their best to educate me. But I feel disappointed with many things, then they said I was good at my grandmother and grandfather. There are many who have had more difficulty in their upbringing.
Its the lack of my parents pesence that feels like a big gap, even though my grandmothers care was bestkind. So are the parents, who are the roots in a childs safety.

My grandmother had probably gastric ulcer, now when she nows how my life had been, not a life after her education.
My parents worked very hard, in order to support us children. My mother worked in my grandfathers company for a while. Then she became like many other mothers housewife, which at that time could be. Though my mother got housewife, I stayed with my grandmother and grandfather, and it is still a question that I never received a reply to. Why they not took me home.
According to my grandmother, so was the reason my mom was offen ill.

Now afterwards, I know shes a hypocondriator which has

a journal thicker than, gone with the wind book. Maybe hard said, but unfortunatly the truth about my mothers progress in healthcare.

My father was a workforce, as I barely know how he looked, when he was almost never at home with his family. He was even less with my grandmother, Ie with her in-laws. Which made me see him very little, has probably been sitting in his knee 10 times during my whole grouth. My father has always had a lot of emotion, nothing he showed at all. They were my grandmother for thousands.

At school I was problem child, I dont want to go to school, I had no friends but was not bullied or exposed, probably I was not a person who burned for school, I feel like a rebellion, went my own way and strangled in others.

You can say, that during my birth, the first seed was empathetic. This seed has evolved throughout my growing up and grown life what I am today. But like all seeds, it must have something that feeds and that makes it grow. Namely to my seed of life, is like in real life a mixture of many ingredients, just like man who eats a nutritions diet. What I want to say is, that there are many things that steered me into the criminal road.

Of course I and 5 other children were allowed to go to the special class, the place school placed messy children, so we did not bother other children. During my adult life, have meet our specialteacher at one time, he then confirmed that the school classified the children by family relationshhip, the richer the better you were considered. If you were a problem child you were nothing worth it. Now 20 years later, he though it was wrong, but that was

the case, right or wrong, what do you think?
When you think how society was at that time, you might wonder how my schooling has come with some other conditions, if the school could help me in an individual and supportive manner, I would have had better opportunity.

But no, its not the schools fault that I entered the crime scene. The thing I want to say is, with better support to develop as an individual, and with a better platform that could be developed into greater work opportunnities, perhaps high school or vocational education helped.

Chapter 2

Although have I today a education in building sheet warehousing. My father made sure I got the education, he employed a vocational teacher from a high school in the field of construction. It was this person who was responsibly for my vocational education.

I worked in my grandfathers company, which my father took over when my granbdfather retired. When I finished my education in sheet metal, that consisted of 6800 hours of education, I worked in the company for a few years, until my dad took my brother into the firm, though he was not interested in working there, but we should have a same salary. It only cost 15 swedish kronor between us, totally wrong, but my dad though it was right. My brother did not know what was up or down the hammer, but we should have same salary. So because of my annoyance on my family, we slipped apart. In the same vein, we moved to another place.

I had to leave the friends I had, and find new ones. May now find out that the move was succesful, but I made some pointless protests. Just then I hated my parents just because, they wanted to change their homes.

The new town was a suburb of Malmö, and there lived a nest cousin to me, and we started to hang out together. It opened up to a new acquaintance circle for me.
There I meet Anna who was a girl in 22 years. She was cute, but I was more or less lucky for her, when she was attending eldery boys, but our roads should be crossed.

One day I went to my nest cousin on my motorcycle, and then I should go home, my motorcycle was gone.
I do not belived my eyes, my bike was stolen. But after 1 our it came a girl driving with it. That was Anna.

She had borrowed my bike to leave a movie as they watched the night before.
She currently had no vehicle, so she took my bike. She said thanks for the loan,
I stood like a tall statue and did not get a sound. I was completely quiet. I was like floating clouds, could only think of Anna.

In the sommer we had a party in my nest cousins house, a party some ended with hes parents thought it out of order. An then when the evening come we fall in sleep in a tent in the garden. When the morning hours came, I wake up to my nest cousin lies on my shoulder all the way.
The reason for it, was at under the night Anna had come into our tent, she lay between me and my nest cousin, and she had only a thin t-shirt who did not keep her breasts in place. Her one breast had come outside the t-shirt. Imagine yourself,
two guys and a nice girl of 22 years with the breasts on the fan. There was still a tent with testosterone stallions in.
It was not straightforward when Anna woke up and wondered if we wanted breakfast, strangely enough neither me or my nest cousin want some food. Anna went to eat, all we wanted was a bag of ice to cool down some body part with.
For Anna was this party, only a party where she asleep in our tent, but for me who was completely in love with this girl, was it not so easy.

I thought she had come to our tent for my sake, but my nest cousin thought she had come for his sake.
Anyway...after a few days, we realized that it was not the case.
Was at a point forced to gone home to my parents, then I could not be at my nest cousin all the time, when I come home I meet my mother and she wondered why I never was at home? I explained that it was summer, and we were out camped like all other youths.

A statement she accepted, went in to pack new clothes, would have to go again the next morning. When I finished, I went out into the garden to keep calm, I meet my father and he wondered why I not had been in work on the whole week?

I explained that I felt unfairly treated, given that my brother had as much as my salary.
My father said we were a family business, and that I could benefit my brother.
My answer to my father was, then my brother could do the same work as me, my dad got angry, and went in and took a beer to be calm, to settle for my answer.
My dad come out again, in the same, moment a friend came to him, they sat down at our garden table with whose beers. I lay in a hammock between two trees. After a while, my mother came to my letter, a pink letter, who had sent me a letter? I oppened it and it stood,
YOU`VE GOT ME ON, and then there was a fishing hook. I did not take anything, probably I was purely proud of my first love letter.

I did not understand what the hook meant, I lay down in the hammock, and look at the letter who someone sent me, when my father wondered who sent it? I dont now!

Was my response to him, and that I did not understand what was meant. Damn...you can read he said, yes I said but I can not understand it. I walked to him, and showed him the letter, my dad screamed straight out...are you stupid? YOU`VE GOT ME ON THE HOOK!

Do you feel well, and my dads friend laughing, I said...I fell well. No I dont beliwed you he said. He asked me if I was in love? Yes I said, but the problem was just that I did not know who sent it. That night I could not sleep, just thought about who could send the letter. All my friends were also curios when I told them about it. Everybody tried to find out who it was, but without results.

One evening, Anna goes to the campsite we were on, and she asked me if I got hers letter? My whole world stopped... ehh yes I stumbled! Good said Anna, because I sent that to you, I was pure pampered... what would I say? She look in my eyes with a light smile on their lips. And her next question was, if I will come home to her in this evening? Yes I said, but where do you live? Right across your house of nest cousin.

Okey... what time? Came when you want, I do a sallad we can eat if you feel like it?

Clearly I wanted to meet, more than well. At 18.00 in the evening, stood in front of her door, had not even bought a flower, probably my age have something to do with it could, barely think in romantic termes. She not came to the door when I called on, I heard a voice that said, come in! Anna stood in the kitchen with the sallad she makes.

Since Anna was living with an elderly person, which was quite so rich, nice furniture and a well stocked bar cabinet, so it became easier to talk to Anna after a couple of rounds to the bar.

The liquor had the advantage of lightening the mood and the evening ended as desired in the bedroom with Anna. It was the same trip the following night,

I started to understand that we had a relationship of the more serious type, might be too serious, because two weeks later comes Anna and tells me, she is pregnant! And she want to keep the kid, I did not know what to answar, I thought with a lump in my throat.

Capther 3

I would be dad? I was only 17 years old, and would
become a parents? Not exactly what I thought, not even in
my wildest imagination, the time stopped completely
for me, I did not get an answar to Anna, who wondered if
I was feeling well? Yes I fell well, but I need to think
about the thing! I went home to think about the matter
and promised, to hear from me later. I really needed to
think about it in peace and quiet, what would my parents
say? And I already had trouble with my father!
Whatever I thought, I did not notice anything that
sounded wise, my dad would probably have a heart
attack. But, as usual, the truth is best in all situations!

Though it may not be easiest to do, to tell you to become
a parent at the age of 17 years for your parents.
In the evening when my father came home after his work
and my mother had the food ready, so I tell them about
one thing that happened, my mother was an anxious
soul, immediately began to think that something terrible
had happened.
Yes, i`ll be daddy, my dad looked at me with a staring
glance, everybody stops to eat.
My dad probably put the food in his throat, because he
started coughing, my mother was cadaverous and they
sade nothing. My mother started to spell out a few
words... **Has it come in there, so let it get out there.**
Then everyone was quiet all night long.

My mother want to speek with me on the morning then my dad has gone to the work, she wondered who the girl was, and why I did not introduce her to them. I tried to explain that everything went so fast, that I did not take it myself, but my mother continued to ask a lot questions that I could not answer. Understood that Anna would meet my parents, it was quite certain, how now it should go, then I knew my mother.

With its embarrassing questions, which could show up at any time. Anna came a few days after I told them, my mother had invited her home and she was curious so she was cracking, my father was calm like a bunker.

Anna came in to the house, and my father started up to talk with her directly, he never used to speak so spontaneously, maybe his way of dealing with the situation.

I was a little shy because they could get, to know each a bit better, and so do not get any hard question. The evening went really well, a success, to my relief.

A more grown-up life began to take shape, though I was only 17 years old, I subconsciously fought against this form of adult life, I wanted to party, and have fun. Anna and I realized that we had to start looking for a home, we should have children in the near future. But to find a home with our income, was not the easiest.

We had to look quite a while and not until three weeks before we were to feed, we received a lease, so we were in a front of a move, personally, I had no furniture, Anna had a sofa, a TV and a little kitchenware. But the worst thing was that Anna was very quick and could not help with the move. My friends and my nest cousin were not counting on them, they lived and motorcycle.

Myself, I had to sell my motorcycle, and buy a stroller with lock-free brakes,
believe that most people may think that there was no major hit, to replace the bike against a stroller.

That I not understood was, I slowly broke down, or rather, my normal personality as a young guy in his best youth year. Clearly I felt bad, but at the same time I thought it would be exciting to be daddy, though I was too young. Time ran out of time, and when I least thought it, Anna started getting the first pain. She became very worried when it hurt so badly. Anna said she could not even imagine such a pain, as she now experienced. We, took decision too call Annas mother, which I barely knew. But she came and pick us up, I had no drivinglicence. So borrowing a motorbike to drive, his pregnant girl to her mother, was not an option.
Anna started to calm down when her mother came into our apartment, Anna was firstborn, and had no experience of giving birth to children.

The only routine we had was the maternity care trials that I and Anna went on a number of times. We got it once! At a maternity meeting, follow a delivery hall in Malmö! The memories I have from that study visit are actually just two! The midwife wanted to breathe in Walter's pace when the pain began! But also the so-called sparkling gas you had to try! It was a real elevator that I would not want to let go of! And there was actually a daddy just laughing! And he did not have a plan to leave it in any way! They could more or less tear it away from him so he could calm down. But as I said! It was the only experience we had. There was one thing that I often reflected on when we were in maternity care. And that was all of the other men

and women involved, as if they were to become parents!
Could have been my parents forever. Many times it felt
very strange to keep up with these exercises as we did!
Felt like there was a tall mommy around one! And not
girls in that sense. It was the age difference that created
this feeling! But now I stood with Annas mother in the
hall and an anxious girl who was going to feed our child!
Something that almost created a form of supernatural
feeling! We had some stairs down and a good bit to the
car. A distance that was done in less than a minute in
normal cases. The stretch became much more difficult
when you have a hard-wearing woman to do! But after
much effort we arrived at the car, and we could only then
sit at her parents and wait for something to happen. It was
a long and good evening. Annas mother thought it was a
false alarm so she was calm! Though Anna jumped up
and down the sofa like an ECG!

Personally, I became nervous about Annas disturbing and
painful behavior! Everything was normal! But I was not
experienced in this area. When it began to approach the
night, the water went full and it became full resurrection.
Everyone ran around like ya chickens and Anna asked me
all the time where that bag was, which she had been
packed for so long. A bag with the most necessary if we
had to go to hospital quickly! Now it was so called sharp
mode and I just wanted to get Anna in the car! Her mother
drove us to the hospital, and we came in time. The wards
made me very nervous! Since I do not like things I can
not influence. Once inside the obstetrics department we
meet a nurse who was quite nice! But with the exception
of her question if the dad was there too, Though I was
standing beside her! Oh what young daddy! Well, I just
thought! It felt like a comment was totally redundant!
Being young was no doubt, but hearing this nurse say so
did I get another thinker about how it really was! The

whole resurrection felt like I was in a bad B movie! And there I figured, as I had a biroll. The nurse told me and Anna's mother that we had to sit down on a bench and wait while they were preparing Anna for the birth! Annas mother who had given birth to several children said that this will take time and that she went home for so long. Well! Are you going to ask me? With a more or less desperate voice! I thought so she said. But wait here! Then you can call me when something started. When Anna came out of the room where they had prepared her. Did she find out that her mom went, then she became both disappointed and afraid. She wanted me to call the friend Anna had been living with before, said and done! Annas friend undoubtedly entered to the hospital, to support Anna. A support I think her mother should have been helpful with. But things rarely come to mind, in this case, it was Anna, in particular, who was betrayed by her own mother. But they have never had a good relationship and it was a lot because Annas mother got a new man and this man became Annas stepfather. A man in total without empathy.

But enough about it! Now it was time to enter the birthplace where our child would be born and I felt how the pulse began to increase dramatically a lot. Oh! What nervous I was! That's how you could almost totally beat. Once inside it became truetaut. I do not know if it was the smell of hospitals or all the technical instruments found in a birthroom! But I was affected by that, there was no doubt! And all the feelings that went through me in a few seconds is something that is almost impossible to describe with words! You must experience it in order to understand how it feels. Anna had to lay on a babybed with a lot of pillows. Anna really had a bad time! It was so that a deaf person could even hear her torments!

For me who stood there LIVE, it was a real thriller! To stand there and not be able to do a joke to make her feel better. I was thinking about what I could do to make it easier for her! But as I said! Then you were almost superfluous! Anna talked more with her friend, even though she had given birth to a child a number of times! And now you can understand a bit better now! I could hardly answer another's questions, regardless of whether I wanted it or not! It was clearly something that women could only answer. But I did my best to assist her. Anna was really aggressive on several occasions! Which was due to her constant recurring contraction. It was not that I was directly jealous of her! Yes! It would be because she had to use nitrous how much she wanted! Or needed! But it would only be for that then! The contraction took a lot and the midwife came in every now and then to see how much Anna had opened!

What I remember would she open 10 cm before her midwife wanted Anna to exploit her aches and thus cry out our child! After 8 hours our child was on our way out! Then suddenly, midwife could no longer hear the baby's pulse! Due midwife calm, I'm not staring at me! When the midwife confirms that the child's pulse is weak! Was not it without my own pulse getting much more excited! The midwife then takes up an electron! Like a sticker with a helical needle in. And at the other end of that needle there was a cord that was connected to an electronic box! This needle should be screwed into the child's head to enable the child's pulse to be recorded. It sounds terrible with no big deal! Without it, it was an easier procedure.

When this electron was in place! we saw the child's pulse on a display, and felt significantly better. I did not know in wisdom one end you should stand in! Anna had said she wants me to film the childbirth! The problem was that

I could not be in two places at the same time! But Anna did not have a better understanding! Then she wanted me to hold her hand for one second! And in the next second she wondered if I filmed? While she said I would film wonder she was the fan I was? I'm filming! You're gonna be here, she screams! Ah I see! Okay! I'm here now! Give me the pleasure gas to give me the sparkling gas!

Everything should apparently be done now! Films you asked Anna! No, I'm here! But you should film that's why we bought the camcorder! I was very close to getting a crush on her frustrated claims, But it was just biting and trying to be as understanding as it just went! Then I knew she was hurt and scared! After much crying, I could now look at our child's head! Seeing that your child is born is an incredible experience that I wish all people could join! When I stood there and watched and filmed! I was completely paralyzed by how a woman's body can bring a child! Incredible! It was no beautiful sight I want to say! When you see how she breaks, the more our child comes out. Honestly she looked like a marinated steak at the bottom. That's how it hurt me! Now the head was out and it was hard to say that a newborn child is beautiful! I have never understood how people can say that! Anna started screaming really damn loudly! I was like a little kid standing there with a camcorder and trembling like a pea pod! The midwife removes the electrode she previously placed there to register the child's pulse! Here comes the child says midwife! The video camera shook like it was a director of Parkinson's disease! My whole body felt like it was dissolved in molecules! The midwife turns to me and says it became a boy, It felt like someone had hypnotized me! Anna was so happy and I was with! Tobias as our child got hot was very hairy!

What made me a little thoughtful about whether it was my

child, Anna had been together with a Greek just before she got together with me! So it was clear that I suspect when the child was very dark and hairy! The midwife comes to me and wonder how I met? Yes, I'm fine, absolutely perfect! She wondered if I wanted to bathe my son? Which, of course, I would! It was going to hell! Then I dropped my son in the baljan where he was going to be bathed! There is no danger said the nurse who helped me! She saw that I was anything but participant! Shocked, I would like to say afterwards. When I had bathed Tobias, I was allowed to lay him down in a small bed on wheels, and drove him to the nursery room where Anna lay down and recovered after childbirth! Anna would get up from bed! Which her friend helped her with! When Anna started to go, it dropped blood on the floor! The midwife comes in at the same time and sees me walking after Anna and wiped the blood on the floor with napkins! She shouts at me! Hello! Yes, I answered! I think you should take me for a while, said my midwife! As I thought would get, paper filled. But that was not the case! She went out with me to get some fresh air! Now sit out for a while and breathe some fresh air, said the midwife! That fresh air could be so good I would never have thought. After a while, Annas's mother came when Anna had called for her. She had not told her mom what it was on the phone! Perhaps it was because she wanted to make sure she really got into BB. When Anna's mother came to the hospital, she saw me sitting there staring straight into the blue! She asks me what it was? I have now learned that I had answered her!

IT WAS A GREEK! Sounds strange! But probably that's when I had my suspicions against Annas last guy who is Grek. Anna would be moved to a maternity ward where they would be a few days. Much because they would see Anna getting breastfeeding and Tobias our son was well.

Still he was all well! What soon became apparent after a few days when he had breast milk and the first surprise in the diaper was delivered to a stranger! I had been home in our flat overnight and came to greet my new family, which had been expanded with a person. Just right till I come! Had my son managed to fill that diaper with some mustard yellow pulp that smelled anything but Hallon! It was an unpleasant experience I can tell. Probably I thought it was extra disgusting because I was so young! Changing his son was not like changing oil on the highway! But I was pretty hot, though it smelled terrible! Soon all relatives came to see the wonders and to congratulate parents. It was very stressful for everyone to come! True that at the same time I would say tolt show off my son! Then it was undoubtedly sometimes difficult. Less difficult it did not happen when the mother lay side about Anna! Coming to us to watch Tobias! So nice little guy you've got! Personally, I was so glad that the tears came! But those tears disappeared quite quickly! When that mother says it's so cute when a sibling gets so moved as I was! What?! Sibling what does that mean stupid mean. And of course I was forced to ask what she meant, Yes! I'll see you tearing a few tears! Hello there! I'm Daddy, Tobias! The mother was completely upset and apologized so much! I then realized that it was hardly the last time I would hear similar comments from outside! After a few days it was time for the family to come home. Tobias would have to sleep in his new bed, which I had screwed up according to all the rules of the art. Like all the other parents, of course, we had a mobile phone on the roof with all sorts of characters that would give our son a calming environment!

There was much to think of, now that you were the parent

and the great responsibility that it meant to be a parent. Anna faced a big change as a person! When she was more mom! And now she had more night time when Tobias would eat every four hours! Of course, this guard made them very joined! The strong mom instinct that Anna got! Did I feel like Daddy? I excluded in any way! Maybe that was just a feeling! But the more joined Anna and Tobias became! The more I felt like dad outside! I think many new daddyes experience this excitement at the beginning! It was like starting a new life! And I and Anna had just been together for a couple of weeks before getting pregnant! When I'm sitting back and thinking! I and Anna never got that time together as all new couples get before deciding to have children!

We should have been together for at least a few years before we even thought of getting children. Then you can easily find that I was too young for this responsibility. As it means to be a parent! I do not regret my children, on the contrary! They are the best things that have happened to me throughout my life. Anna and I did what we could for our family to have it as good as it just went! Many relatives would come with so-called good advice! Annas mother was probably the one who walked the least with the pointer! Because that's probably my mother's mind! Which created conflicts between Anna and my mother! It could be quite awesome for those days when Anna just said what she thought of my mother! Then my mother was violated according to what she herself said! But it did not require much to get her nose in the weather!

Chapter 4

Yes, it was like my whole world had been rubbing out!
And now you only had to adjust as much as you could!
Strange it is! But adapting you actually do! Do you have
small children, then get sharp and do not hesitate on a
trifle when problems come and go every day! A problem
that is certainly very common! Is that sex life one can
look after in the blue! Anna was anything but interested in
our sex life! But it was me! Are you 17 years old, you
wake up with the blanket in the roof every morning
without a problem! But believe me! There was nothing I
had any use of! Of course, I can now understand it a bit
better. But to be 17 years old, then you need to say that! I
could eat the loss if I did not get sex! But as much as I
needed, Anna did not want it. That was a pretty big
problem for me! Many women do not feel fresh when
they are breastfeeding and they have been forced to go
around with the aftermath! So sure, I can now understand
it a bit better! Tobias grew well and he was completely
healthy. You really should be happy! When we learned
later that someone in the prophylaxis group had a girl
with spina bifida which is not an uncomplicated disease
or disability. So compared to that, our problems appear to
be extremely small! But you stand closest to yourself. I
worked on my father's days, though it was against! I was
whipped to raise money for the family when it was
expensive with children and constantly new expenses!
Anna was at home with Tobias for a whole year before
she started working a little extra! She had her regular
work at the post office, which yielded a secure income.
Though we had two incomes, we could not save any
money. Should you get a little over a month, they

Disappeared in the next month. We never had any money for any pleasure! Though I worked extra, they disappeared without any problems. And then our life continued for several years! My income was bad and Anna started talking about Tobias a sibling! A sibling that would mean we had to move! But with my income, no bigger accommodation would be anything alternative. Anna began to talk to me that I would ask for a salary increase with my father! Just to hear word wage increase was almost laughing! Then I knew my father, who would not raise my salary! But I actually asked my dad about it. But the answer was, as I said, no to that question!

Having a girl who would have a sibling and a low income! Be prepared for a conflict! For a while, Anna forgot it with siblings and nobody was happier than me! After a few more months it was like a biological bell reminded her of just one sibling! We both agreed that we did not have enough large apartment for a child to! But also that we did not have wages that could cover a larger living space! The situation began to become unsustainable! And something had to be done! I initially hoped that Anna would realize that it would not go! Then our conditions were completely wrong! Raising a child to now would mean major changes and demands on larger incomes! We thought about a few weeks and the best we could get! Where to start your own business so that I could get a few thousand pieces more this month. But all who are or have been own entrepreneurs already know that this was no brilliant proposal! If you want to make money, then you, as your own business owner, more or less get to, work around the clock! To make it go! Even myself should realize that when I grow up in business homes. It was not a coincidence that both my grandfather and father were working 24 hours a day! But in some way, it was that you did not take that information, or I would not realize it! Then I probably hoped it would be quiet in my own family and that Anna would have the long-awaited child! Apparently her mother's identity completely screamed after. Now I may think it sounds ridiculous! Starting your own business! So we could change housing and get a sibling to Tobias! But life is obviously a difficult case to solve! But that's the challenge of life! And there is, not always the intention to predict life. Even though you could sometimes wish it! The decision was taken! I and Anna start their own company in building sheet warehouse. The fact was that I was on the paper, and I was the main responsibility of the company! Which maybe was pretty given then I was the customer profession. It was not a big idea to let Anna stand on it! As she said, she worked in the mail! Due to the fact that I opened my own company in building sheet warehouse, it created a major conflict between me and my father! That was very disappointed with me! Because he had thought I would take over his, business! As it's so called. True conflicts and hate speech were spoken between him and me! It even went so far that my own father was talking about me! Out on the building where he was and worked.

Much of his bad ways was probably due to the disappointment that my father now knew! Certainly, I can understand him to some extent! But he knew at the same time that I went to his company underpaid! And that I needed to change housing! Honestly, he could have raised my salary a few thousand, a month! But my dad saw it with other eyes. I worked hard for my company to go around and to create a large customer base! With my dad in the heels! Which did not directly pave the way for me in any way!

On the contrary! Everything was difficult at first when I would contact wholesalers and they asked for references, though they knew who I was! And that I had been in their stores and made many times. But they had their obligations to check out new companies that started shopping in their company! My company was new and with some references. But it was only to start, shopping in cash and after half a year, went shopping for 30 days invoice.

I was very careful to pay in all the invoices as fast as it went. My customers had to pay in 15 days and it was not always as it went! Then my company sometimes worked towards larger companies and was used to pay in 30 days. Then the check credit went hot i would say! I was in an extremely vulnerable state all the time, and prayed for a prayer that the companies paid their bills! So I managed to push the invoices, which was not quite unusual to do in the construction industry. True, I basically knew the prerequisites in the industry! I never drew a second to start my business! Sure, there was a lot of excitement, opening up a company and just as much worries about how it would go! Again, I think my low age had its part in this matter! Then I did not have a lot of life experience. Anna was older than me and maybe I wanted to be in a pathetic way, show me that I was enough to run my own business! But that's the case! His proud manhood would show up! Though it actually shone with its great absence! Anna certainly had expectations for both me and the company! That was a positive result in the wallet, which was the reason I started my own business. A company that was supposed to solve our big problems! It began to roll in large sums of money from the work that my company had performed.

I often thought that there were unbelievable sums that you got the pleasure, of billing. What I forgot was! That it For the most part, the supplier's money and VAT were later bitterly payable to suppliers and to the state. My company managed to get a lot of work! And it was fun for my family, who had been worried about how it would go! Not least for my mother who often rang to hear if everything was good! My father did not call. But I hardly figured that man would bend his neck and be happy for me! No, it seemed like he thought it was better to be bitter. So just let him sit there and sour! If he now thought it was fun!

My family's life rolls on like usual! But I and Anna did not have much time for each other, when my life was mostly at work! And it's a common syndrome with new entrepreneurs. You do not have the social network around you that you have when you are employed! Being sick was hardly an option as a sickness compensation would be very low per day. It's well the back of being your own business owner! I wanted to rate as low income as possible. Ideally, it would go plus minus zero when everything was paid. Now I had more F-tax, which meant that I paid the same tax, regardless of whether I had income for a month, or not! The job did not seem to end in any way.

Anna and I decided to buy a house! Then we felt more covered now, for a larger living! And we were also faced with getting another family member! Anna was pregnant again! And she was very happy about it! I was also happy! But there were a lot of other things that I thought I had to find out! The job had increased a lot, and, as I said, I was working in the company myself. Hiring a person would cost a lot, and I did not know how long the work orders would arrive at the pace it has done lately. I only had two options! ither, I had to hire a person or cancel my job! But as a new entrepreneur, a no wouldn´t sound that good to a customer, so I decide to hire a guy on an appointment! I did not dare to hire a full-time person.

Now it was not just a lot of work, but at the same time I had to find a good guy who could do his job and not only write sick as soon as the person in question had an issue! But where do you find such a person? I felt a lot of pressure! And though I was not that old, was not the requirements less for it. Anna tried to assist with the recruitment as much as she could. She was more like a support, because I would feel less pressure! But not a fan, I felt less pressure! The few hours I was away from the building the phone went hot. Customers do not want to wait for their turn. All work ordered on the day would be better on the day before! An impossible mission in other words! After a lot of work, I found a younger guy who had gone to the building line. He was not a record maker, but he seemed to be able to do something about building, it worked quite well with that guy! As I now helped, it was really what the boy's work was, to help me keep things where you had to be two.

Anna had begun to get really fat and there was not much time left until she would be born our second child! This became like a worry in my everyday life! I could not be home because it would cost too much, and the job could not wait! I had hoped Anna could feed one Friday after 4:00! That would have been great! No no! She could not do it! She would feed in the middle of the week when it was the most to do! I had acquired a searcher, so she could Search me when it was time for a trip to the hospital.

I started to get routine in this area! But as they usually say, Is it never a birth like the other? I just got to the hospital, then it was clear! It was a bad speed this time. But it was not more than 2 years in between the births! And they usually say that you will not be restored as a woman from the first seven years after the last birth! Anna was not worse at her. After birth we were now four in the family. A family with two guys! Anna had hoped for a little girl, but it became a real Swedish boy this time! I thought that was absolutely perfect. One had their ideas that it was easier with boys. But that science built most of what the men in the building had said in the breaks! And probably was the best thing! Maybe it's easier when the kids are in the teens with a guy. But there are other problems with guys.

My work continued, and the guys grew good, So I had nothing to complain about. Maybe a little bit of cohabitation! Between me and Anna. But forming a family and starting companies had their backs! But you also have a human ability to feel sorry for yourself, On that question, I'm not an exception! Anna wanted to renovate our house, which in some places was more than necessary. I thought we would renovate the garage roof that had begun to leak. We came up with a double-rolled plate roof! Then it would raise the value of our house and be a good investment for the future. I even put up the panel in the kitchen to refresh it a little, and a black plate roof on the garage so everyone could be happy. The guy working on my company was really reliable and I really got a great deal of trust for him, in every way! He always stood up and worked! Whether it was weekend or everyday! I was thinking about firing him up.

Chapter 5

Then that absolutely did not happen!
Two customers had not paid their invoices. I immediately
contacted these customers and wondered why these
invoices have not been paid? A customer replied that they
would check my company's work before the invoice was
paid. Then they pointed out that it only took 15 days on
the invoice. I began to wonder why they suddenly began
discussing the number of days on the invoice, I started to
feel that something else was wrong. But at the same time,
I would not believe it! There was enough fear when I got
these thoughts. The next day we were on a bigger
building, where I knew you were always paid for their
work! It could take a little longer than 15 days! Before I
got paid! But always paid. When breakfast came, we went
down to the store that the builder had put there to the
workers, and there me and the guy the guy even ate our
breakfast.

We sat there and discussed a lot of different things when
another craftsman regretted that he had not been paid by a
customer! It turned out that it was the same customer that
I had not been paid for! Imagine the world is small! The
entrepreneur told us that he had a very large amount
invoiced to this particular customer, and he was worried
that the invoice would never be paid! This entrepreneur
was a well-established entrepreneur and was worried! Did
I really have reason for my concern!

It became a time of uncertainty, which became worse than
anyone could imagine! It turned out that the other
customer who had not even paid his invoice was more
complicated and was basically about a customer who had
put it in a system of not paying! The customer claimed

property. Which I knew was completely wrong. I even proved it by contacting the namely that my company had caused a greater water damage in their basement, when we reaffirmed their municipality.

Because I saw that there was a very old water damage on the wall down in their basement, did I want a surveyor to check the alleged water damage that the customer claimed that my company caused. The customer took your inspector and I also took your mine. Thus, we would have two statements independent of each other. Even when the surveyors would check the amount of moisture it was in the walls! Then their instruments barely made any difference at all. All basements have some moisture and are quite normal. The customer's inspector informed the customer that it was normal with this moisture, which allowed the customer to start mistrusting his own selected inspector. My company inspector could only say the same as theirs! To describe what it looked like on the spot, one could say that there was a small cellar with a low ceiling. On the basement walls what it painted with some olive green, plastic paint that had burst and had let in from the walls. The paint that had been released was so dry that you could break it with your fingers and it does not speak directly because the basement would have recently been water-damaged.

The inspection continued into an adjoining room in the basement where the customer had his laundry in that room not only the color had dried, but the wall from the wall had also fallen down. To the point belong! The fact that the customer had pointed out that the damage caused by my company was in the previous room where the moisture was almost nonexistent.

But in the room, we now entered, there were significantly higher values like the surveyors could register with their instruments! But though the values were higher, it was due to an old injury and it was both the viewers' views. Because their opinions were so similar, I thought that the customer would now pay his invoice.

But not! No, they took your inspector. A person who later appeared to be related to the customer. Of course, he claimed that the damage had occurred due to the fact that the pipes had been removed while we mounted a new hangover for the daylight. When disassembling an existing drain pipe to drain the water into the ground! If you install a temporary hose that, in the meantime, fulfills the same function as a drip tube, do the usual cases. My customer then claimed that the temporary snake had been released during the weekend and that there was a lot of rain that weekend. It was just crazy! Now I began to get angry. I myself was hunted for paying the suppliers for the material they delivered to this particular building.

Now I stood before a long and destructive time! Where my company had to send reminders to the customer and who would later go to the crown court. The customer then turns to a lawyer in order to get the right in his case. I knew we had not caused this damage to their property. But now I had to turn myself into a legal person!

To meet the customer. The customer was given legal aid in this matter. I did not get it! Then I was a trader! Although there was some help getting from the National Organization, it seemed that I would have to pay the biggest part myself!

Now I was really faced with big problems. Would I tell Anna about what had happened, No! I made a decision to wait for it when we had just had children and she had been sleeping bad lately. Giving Anna such a message would only make her more sleepless, which was absolutely unnecessary! Right now, I was living with a hope that everything is going to be alright. Certainly, I regret now that I did not tell Anna directly about what had happened. But I just wanted my family to feel good, with all that meant! All the problems that have arisen now! Did it happen that I suddenly had to live some kind of double life! Then I did not tell her about what happened! Yes! You are doing many custom things when you get into these situations.

You have a human survival instinct, where you would like to be in some form of denial of truth. The problems just seemed to get lost! And as you usually say! An accident seldom comes alone! So, it was in my case too! Then it turned out that even the other customer who would pay after 30 days at the end did not have coverage for the jobs he had ordered. We were three different companies who incurred huge losses. The more worked-up companies had during the years had a buffer of liquid funds. But my company got much bigger problems! I had to try to explain what happened to Anna! That day the thoughts went my mind, how would I explain that to her? That two customers have not paid their invoices! I did not want to worry about her, but now I just had to inform her about this problem. Very right, she became worried about this

and began to discuss that she would pick up the customers. Which would not be so good, as there were already lawyers on these matters! But to see her despair, completely tear me apart! We who had been so good and the boys that felt so good.

Would all our life just go to the woods now? Just because two customers did not pay. Many times, you forget the mental pressure that gets when you get financial problems with this caliber! It clearly touched us on every level! And those wears that occurred then became like a big open wound between me and Anna! And as I usually say! The wound heals, and the crust draws off! But the scar consists.

Of course, the scars also fade over time. But time was something that neither I or Anna had, what we had there against! Be authorities and wholesalers who would get paid by us, or rather, by my company. It started to be a big gap between me and Anna. Which, in turn, began to lead to the disagreement between us, when it was a lot of money, The total loss was just over a hundred and a half! An amount that is large when the company was restarted, I desperately began to redistribute the available amounts that the company had. I had to wait with the VAT, so I could pay the wholesalers. Without the wholesalers, I had not had any material to work with. Then I had to postpone business tax. Then I start pushing the treasure, where the guy would get his salary! He would not have to suffer because customers did not pay. I did not want somebody to suffer! Desperate as I was! Then I thought that everything would solve! Only it became a settlement in an arbitration tribunal. Yes, it's absolutely amazing that you can be so fucking naive to believe such a stupid thing.

Anna was actually less naive than I was! She said quite early that this will not solve, in any good way! I myself was quite convinced that it would be fine.
I received despite all the problems and stresses continue to work around the clock. I tried to work out the losses, which was completely impossible! It became like the whole company came out of phase. I deliberately submitted cheaper quotes for the jobs I counted on! In

order to get more jobs that could cover the losses. It was an impossible mission that no would have succeeded! But then I still weary almost 24 hours a day.

Now it was time to meet the customers in the arbitration tribunal to get things right. I thought! That was not the case. One customer lacked total payment ability and there were others who stood before me to get paid. Especially banks! So that trial ended with having done a good job, but the customer lacked total payment options! So my company did not get a crown. Not easy when there is no measurable property. In pure Swedish I was not paid for my work. As for the other customer who claimed that my company had caused moisture in their basements. Then, as mentioned, the customer had turned to a further inspector who had confirmed their claim, and as we claimed was wrong! And that they had a relationship through their relationship. What the right should be regarded as Jäv. My company's defense had even checked with the municipality more carefully if the municipality had had any leaky pipes at that time. What was documented and presented in court. The district court nevertheless went on the plaintiff's history and meant that the reason was due to the snake that had jumped off during the rainy weekend and that was the cause of the damage!

The customer would have called me! Then they saw that the water was running the furthest façade! When my defense felt that the couple should try to put on the throat again! To prevent their perceived damage. The right meant that the customer would be considered a layman and I was a skilled worker. Because I lost in the district court.

Chapter 6

I thought I'd be crazy! We had two impartial inspectors who confirmed that my company was innocent! But also a good documentation from the municipality that they had a big leak a few years earlier, as so many homeowners in that street had been affected by! Honestly! Do not I understand today how they could judge that! When I and my lawyer felt that our evidence was absolutely huge! But apparently they could do it. My lawyer said that we should appeal to this! Yes, that sounds easy! But being in process, is not directly free, because lawyers cost a lot. I understood in that second that now it was running! And it's really good! Anna would get a cramp when she found out this. But she had the right to know it, though it did not matter!

Total loss! Be now a fact and it was also our relationship as it stormed heavily around when Anna wanted me to do something about it. But what could I do? Only to realize the loss, What else could I do? Anna thought we would contact the bank in order to raise the current check credit! In other words, she wanted us to lend us out of the problem. Loans are definitely no solution if you have such issues as we had. Which one bank had quickly found and therefore I did not consider it a good solution! The thoughts began to become destructive at all levels, and the desperation that I now felt was heavy to bear! Now it felt like hell broke out and just everything had gone to hell! It's even so that, after all these years, I remember how bad I felt, now that you sit here writing these lines. Yes usch! Anna was as changed! And it's hard to blame her for it. I started working more and more black. Which did not directly benefit my family or business. Anna was disap pointed that I became so passive when I no longer cared about my company. It was as I had given up in total and just arranged so that we could live well without paying taxes! I had become hateful to society because of these very sick trials that made my company completely out of action! It is usually said that revenge is the world's oldest motive! Nowadays, I can really say with conviction that I was extremely vengeful to everything and everyone outside my family! I started to mistrust just everything. I just did what fell in! No one could influence me in my decisions, I was tired of being kind to everything and everyone. Now it was me who ruled my own ship! My own ship can be said that it was shortly after, when Anna wanted to separate.

She meant, that she did not feel like breaking down, she did not think we had a good relationship either! But all the fairy tales do not always have a beautiful end! It did not have our relationship, nor would I promise. We started the company together and I made sure our family had everything it needed. But when everything went to the woods, Anna did not want to know of my company, but just wanted to move and I would take a break at all levels! She was not panic about how life would be, she was not alone in being. But she was terribly determined at that point and it was absolutely impossible to discuss this subject with her! Anna wanted us to live apart and that we would jointly sell our house. Well! Now we should clearly sell the house we once did to buy! But we were both on the house and I did not want to sell, I had to unleash her! Which It was not a good option when my company had the big loss in my luggage. But asking Anna to await the move, like asking the church to stop saying Amen! The hatred between me and Anna began to grow significantly and soon I was in a new conflict with lawyers who would divide our housing and equipment.

Our children had even noticed that something was wrong between Dad and Mom! Which made our little son Alexander often sad. He always wondered where one was somewhere! Although I and Anna had a conflict, we did everything for our children to not hear us when we broke. But it's not always easy when you get angry and disappointed with your partner. The children always get in some way when the parents decide to separate. I felt that I was no longer the kind and thoughtful person I once had. I was ashamed every time my big boy Tobias ask why mom should move! He often wondered where dad would live, and they get the words my son said to me, like a knife straight into the marrow on me! I felt a terribly uncomfortable feeling of betrayal to my own children. And the tears were impossible to hold back, how can I forgive myself? At the same time, I had to defend myself purely mentally by thinking of these two customers who did not pay their invoices and that was actually the root of all the evil! But explaining for his own child that dad's business had been fooled on big sums of money was no, alternative. They were simply too small to understand such a thing! Many of my thoughts were how to get out of this misery. The more time passed and I saw how Anna packed their stuff became the most idiotic thoughts, suddenly completely brilliant plans! Man is strange that way! One begins to think and act like the worst cave man. I just wanted to go home to those customers and explain with a ball tree what I think and make sure they paid. But I was still too civilized to do something like that! But then I thought that such an act could solve the problem! I did not see any sanctions that such an act could end! But thank fully I did nothing, Believe, that my children made me think of other thoughts. I did not want to miss them because I would have done something wrong. But to say that those thoughts did not exist had been a lie.

Anna would start moving in with her mother for a few weeks until she had a groundfloor. I wish she would stay with me until it was time to move in. I did not even think of the idea that my children would not be home in our house. Totally cracked I was! Felt like I would break up and I think I could do anything for my family to stay whole! When you love your family! Suddenly, it was as I stood for all the feelings in the family. Then I mainly think of Anna. The children always show their feelings. They were often sad about what would happen! Nothing could I do! More than accepting that I was now without the family and would soon be sitting in a house! All the paintings that filled their place and all the memories with them were like gone! Some paintings were left, but it felt very empty! Suddenly things were never taken care of before! But only now they had been worthy of gold. They were a memory! All the trouble made you feel kluven. Anna, whom I loved so much! Hate me as much now, if not more!

Chapter 7

Now it was time to wave his family! Tears completely faded down on my cheeks! I did not wipe them away and I did not care about it either! I shook my whole heart of the grief I felt! Because that was exactly what it was! Sorrow! I had lost my family in some way. My kids screamed in the back of the car as if they were going away. If you never had such a parting, it's hard to understand how emotionally charged it is. I was a shattered man to say a bit!

I just stood there and saw how my children disappeared from me! It was like pulling the plug into a bathtub full of water. Everything that I stood for just ran away in a few seconds. I felt completely emotional and just at this moment! Did not it matter if the whole world was gone! It was enough that my world had gone underneath. Being sad while feeling totally emotional was something that worried me a lot! Mentally, it felt like my body was about to split into two different parts! It was like having the evil angel on one shoulder! And the good angel on the other. What was happening to me? It was extremely hard to feel so. I had an education, one had learned to be a good and kind person. But that was anything but what I felt now! While all the good disappeared from me! Did it feel like something bad and phantom filled in in the other part of me? I was tired of all the heavy decisions between me and Anna had to push on my company, though that was the last thing I wanted to do. The guy working with me had a month's notice and he had to terminate. Felt like a further betrayal on my part! The guy was prepared for it and just had to be unemployed for a few days. But it still felt so wrong. My company had to pay a final salary to him, but also a vacation allowance. The company's cashier was hard hired, and I had to pay a salary to myself! Then I had a lot of costs on the house! The loan we shared, we stood for half each, so it felt a bit better! But then it was the most, crazy rest. My company had a so-called Hangover Agreement with the union, which had to be in order to be able to work with major entrepreneurs, as they were thoroughly affiliated! This Hangover Agreement was also a form of guarantee for other entrepreneurs and individuals that the companies fulfilled the requirements that existed on companies with employees. The agreement would also give the indication that the company was not just a so-called "company in pocket" which was good in this industry.

Now that everything else had collapsed, the union would be paid for all of these fees, which existed through this agreement! As my company had signed several years ago. But now they were not as nice to have to do with it! Like when I sign the agreement! Due to the fact that my company had a lot of other expenses, then this union fee was something that just had to wait. They could not imagine in any way, though they knew what my company had been through! After a few months of unpaid fees to the union, I received a call for a district court hearing. When I come to the District Court, I sit with the Ombudsman with whom I once signed the agreement. He barely said hello! But when he signed the agreement, he had a pastry with him! But now we sat in the middle of each other and looked closely at each other, as we have always been unfaithful. Now we were called for a rule that was extremely small. No major negotiation there not. Just an elongated table with chairs, then a bench of a little coarser model where the referee sat with a secretary.

The referee asks me if I intend to pay these fees. I replied that I would do as soon as there was an economic opportunity for this. The union representative then tells the judge that they can only see a deal during the day otherwise the union would like my company to be bankrupt with immediate effect. The referee asked me again! But supplement their direct question if I wanted to pay it today. I replied that there were significantly more important things my company needed to pay, such as suppliers. The union mediator was completely untouched. The judge was sitting with a pencil in his hand, I remember that! He sat there and spin and spin it back and forth. A pen that would symbolize a chairman's club. After a brief discussion between the judge and the secretary, the judge decided to put my company in bankruptcy because they thought my company was in insolvency as it is so called. In other words! A judge puts my company in bankruptcy. My company I had worn my hedge for. The referee looks at me and then hits the pencil that he had in his hand during the whole hearing in the table! As such, both set the judgment and end this debate. There I sat and was totally humiliated to a maximum by a judge who was at least 60 years old and a representative from the union who did not seem to show the least understanding. Any entrepreneur who had the choice to pay his suppliers or trade union had chosen the suppliers. Without any suppliers, you were out of the market anyway. The union could give a longer standstill with these payments. There was hardly any need at the trade union. But it was just about pure abuse of power where they would show that you do not bother with the tray. Many entrepreneurs encountered the actual union abuse that, under the law, completely crushed entrepreneurs who did not dance after their pipe! I was not on that issue particularly unique! When many had gotten their unconscious power in our society. Wondering if I could get farther down the bottom of society.

Then I had lost everything in my life. Without even being the least stringy. My life had been totally broken by many factors. Maybe I should have acted differently. Yes, it's hard to know! Then I no longer saw any opportunities or any brighter future. I was now around 22 years old and was already totally driven into society. My young age made them destructive thoughts, began to gain a power all around my personality! What just before was horrendous thoughts began to create a whole new person. A person who was cast in a shell of lead. A casing that guaranteed not to emit any emotions. I began to feel a hatred within me! That would not initially come out, out of this, lead apron human body. Angry got a brand new, face for me! And as soon as one society would get acquainted. The same community that has been with and created this ice cold, emotional call person! I, who had barely been driving red light throughout my life, now faced a whole new life! A very destructive life. It is usually said that it is a wait or anxiety that is difficult. The thoughts went to my boys that I could not support. Everything was gone! Many may think how to be so stupid, that you become a criminal. To you I just want to say! That you stop your eyes for a second and think if someone has taken away your life. Do you as a person do your utmost to be both a good father and a good citizen as a trader. Questions that arose in my head were, why all this crap would happen to me and my family. Was this fate? Hardly! But some sense must have had, though those purposes were extremely impossible to interpret. Some people believe that one can control fate to some extent. That's something I'm skeptical about!

Then I see how my own life has looked the last 15 years. What could I do? To so-called, controlled my destiny? It would have been that I skipped the criminal bit in my life. But that sounds easy and it was anything but what it was.

If you stand without a future, you will get a future, whether it's good or bad. Only I could survive. Many wondered where my conscience had taken the road? My conscience had begun to leave me. When it comes to ethics and morality, what's the end of a piece. My old I started to gradually erase, slowly but surely.

Anna noticed that I had changed extremely much. She does not like what she saw more now. But what was Anna so up to? According to her! Did she feel that my action by manipulating the VAT forms made me guilty of crimes, but that was history now! I did not have my business left. Why pick it up now? When I did, she did not cheat when the VAT money came to us. I do not believe what you say, I answered her! Then she says I worked black to one hundred percent! And that was true, what she said now! But I could not see it as a major crime, when I asserted that half Sweden does it every day. But now I realize that these BLACK JOBS were one step closer to the crime. By justifying tax-free work, you begin to accept lawsuits. Even though it is an easier form of crime, it is an introduction to the crime scene. Even if it sounds stupid, the human brain begins to get used to accepting what's wrong. I began to lie both for myself and for my environment. The lies are one denial that assists one, in order not to be bad, of what you do! Rather than taking a headache tablet that is pain relieving. But the truth is unfortunately another. Do you lie or take painkillers, just lurking your own brain to believe that the pain is gone, but everything in life is connected in one way or another, just as the pain-relieving medicine is over, it's just as safe that you'll soon have to create another lie to cope with your life! And cover up with the lie you said before. It was not just Anna who had noticed my new destructive behavior. No all of our previous common acquaintances, as our friends had even noticed it now. Friends who had children of the same age as we. They did not say much at first when they did not want to go down and even less involved. They were surprised! Did Anna tell me! That they were astonished, I could understand when they felt like a kind and very caring person. One person could call the middle of the night if they needed help. There were even those friends who thought I had a milder form of psychosis. Then my new behavior was like the difference between day and night. That I probably was shocked at how everything had gone to hell I do not doubt myself. But it was not a psychosis. No! I would like to say that it was a built-in human survival instinct. An instinct that grew destructively stronger for each day that went. That I could not see it myself! Now, after all, is a horrible thought that I just want to forget about. Anna knew I would not put my children at risk. That's something she never blamed for. But being destructive thinking on the weekends and then being daddy on the weekends was a challenge. The children often ask what Dad is working with. What should you answer? Daddy is probably a criminal damn! No! No good suggestion right away. The children were still quite small. Which meant they did not stand one against the wall with theirs issues. But having to lie for their own children did not matter in every way! The feeling, that I had begun to be a bad father began to come crawling. A feeling I did everything to deny, when it simply became too hard to think about! I felt bad of just the thought. I'm a good father I thought thousands of times! Then I darkened my bad side purely mentally.

It was the kids who held their nose over the water surface. Tobias, my big son was born with bad hearing! Which meant many days in hospitals and where hearing tests were to be conducted and later caused him to be operated! They operate in small tubes in his ears. They made sure to drain the fluid that was filled behind his mucous membranes. Because he had it from birth, this was his speech quite powerful! Then he was basically deaf. Anna and I only discovered it when he was watching a cartoon on television. He almost always had it at the highest volume. My minor son suffered from the same problem, but there we could check it earlier, when we knew it was likely that he had it! The doctors said the children were growing from this problem, which was correct.

That my children needed his father there was no doubt about that. They would like to say on different controls occasionally. But combining my wild me with being an available dad was not the easiest task. Like many other criminals, I did everything to hide the bad side. But I had not come to the conclusion that I was a criminal. I probably saw myself more like a living artist. But my surroundings, say, relatives and friends had another idea about that. Many asked what I was living on. My answers were always the same. FAITH, HOPE and BAD WITH LOVE! Yes, you hear how bad it already sounded. But man is a virgin and the fact is that after 21 days you get used to it, whether it's something you like or not! But so is actually man funted. What do I want to tell you then? Well, I am programming myself to accept what was happening, though it was pure hell. I changed my mind unconsciously and slowly flowed into my new costume. Since I used to work a lot when I was a self-employed,I started to get restless, and there was another warning sign. I was a workforce already at that time. The problem was just that I had no job. But I had a lot of hate, revenge and

50

a lot of other crap inside, who now more aggressively tried to penetrate the lead-dressed personality that I had now developed into! That's all the crap wanted out at one and the same time. At the same time, I was a cautious person, maybe the kind Angel had not completely abandoned me. But the evil was the stronger. Which I began to notice, because I no longer felt so bad of my destructive thoughts and ideas. I started wondering how to get a payback on society that I thought would have left me in the shit! Now it was time to give up twice!

I have always been very interested in technology. The music has also had a big part in my life, now I have played the piano for 29 years. But even computers have been something that I've always burned for.

Unfortunately, I did not take the opportunity when, as a young musician, I got a good offer. No! Then there were only jobs and computers in question. But suddenly I began to realize what a computer could do for effective things. I thoroughly worked on analyzing different computer systems, the front of all systems was no longer as interesting, then I was very committed to the hearts of the systems. I simply wanted to see the source code for those different programs that were now very interesting.

Most computer systems do not have an open source code. And the source code was the back of the different programming front where everything happened. The backside was so interesting that I started reading about language. If you have never seen a source code, I can tell you that, at first sighting of these source codes. Is as messy and insensitive as seeing a written document in Latin. You only see a lot of characters that you do not understand the least of. It was like reading an encrypted text pulp in Marsian.

But despite these insensible signs and points, I was determined to learn this language. I would initially learn to understand the meaning of these signs, I started reading books about a programming language called C +. An extremely sophisticated programming language and later called C ++. It made me almost crazy when I did not understand a shit. But I did not give up for it. Then I'm an extremely stubborn person.

I began to contact people who share my great passion! Data! But when I explained what I was doing, they were more or less willing to drive me to YELLOW DELIVERY! To the psyche in other words. When they considered learning that language was a huge work and that there was no reason to do that. I would hardly seek work as a programmer. But I had completely other plans for the learning language of programming languages. I wanted an outlet for my revenge request. As I write these lines, I realize how wrong I was. But that was how I thought and, not least, acted. What I've done was wrong! But that's exactly what this book is about.

Those days that I did not have my kids, I engage in one hundred percent of reading and learning, so much I only hurried about this new and black hacker world. A future retaliation tool that I did not draw the least to learn. This revenge feeling was so huge! So, I was more or less forced to enforce all these thoughts on revenge. But before the revenge would come! Should I know how to handle this effective weapon to one hundred percent. t is now known that violent crime is often based on impulsive actions while the economic crisis is usually based on planning. Now this is not general but pure average. But considering what I've been doing for almost 15 years! Then I know that eco-robbery is not based on impulsive decisions. We leave the theoretical piece.

Throughout my teaching period you went on a lot of unnecessary bangs, mistake I had to regret many times. But exercise gives you skills. However, it is associated with a lot of costly and embarrassing exercises. But giving up this payback was no alternative. The driving force I was wearing was strong and persistent! A perseverance like never under the age of 15 weakened the smallest. Then you might better understand how strong my hatred was. When I after some time began to get accustomed to how these different programming languages worked, it was like a pure poison.

Chapter 8

I analyzed and analyzed until the eyes blew. For a while I was in it! So, I saw the source code only I blew. All of this information I gathered on me, and then started creating small applications or in plain language! Small program. These small programs had no major features. But it was undoubtedly a kick when you got these codes to roll as a program, though it had no purpose at that time. I started making bigger programs to see if I could make it work! Most times, the forest was cleaned. But it was only to continue until it worked.

Now, many people wonder what it was like to sit and try to do a lot of different small programs as there was no sense with that, the reason for this was to learn how programs were built and what weaknesses differed system had. For fact, no program is 100 percent safe. All systems and programs have a weakness! It only applies to finding the weakness. An enormous time-consuming job. To everyone, like some kind of movie, it's about getting into a system and there is someone who tries to break the system by writing a lot of different passwords. I can tell you, that does not work. All these combinations amount to millions and are totally impossible for the human brain to handle. It would be if the person is lucky and succeed in writing the correct password. But reality is a completely different one. Highly sophisticated applications require different combinations. Such a program can take several days through weeks, and if it's bigger servers you can crack it may take months!

That I did these small programs was to get the knowledge about how to create viruses. Many do not know that a virus, in fact, is a small program, and its small task is to carry out some illegal actions. Learning to create entry paths in the different systems was goal one. Many systems are protected today by firewalls. But as I said! Everything goes if you just want to.

There are some easier ways to get into different systems. But it's based on knowing some prerequisites for just what you want to get into. Many system developers are programming what is called backdoors in their own system. A form of security for the author or company to never be excluded from its own product. Which would be terrible! But these backdoors are unfortunately a security risk that the customer is never aware of. Thus, most companies purchase a product of well-established companies claiming their system is very secure. But it's not safer than the manufacturer can get in, whenever they want! Just to give an example of this is the Windows operating system. An operating system that many individuals and companies use in their daily lives. The fact is that each license to an operating system has a series. And each series of these operating systems has a gold key. This gold key does not tell the manufacturer. It's so bad! That you can easily download these gold keys via the Internet. So sure! You can never be when you usually have a computer in your everyday life. But as I told you, man can not handle or combine all these millions of different passwords and usernames. Therefore, my goal was to create different kinds of small programs or viruses that a regular person had perceived as. Getting into someone else's computer! Be a prerequisite for being able to empty it on their most important information.

But in order to get this information I had to get in unnoticed. Getting in via the internet was not a simple match at the start. Then the Internet consisted of connection via the regular phone. What most people know meant that you had to dial a phone number. A so-called modem pool number and many did not have the AXE system connected to their phone. Which meant that one could only be one on the line. Many homes had to shut down to make regular calls. Which did not make it so easy to get in! Many attacks were carried out at night when most people slept. Then the next problem was to solve. People often shut down their computers at night. So, it was in the beginning.

Today with broadband is usually the computers around the clock! Then many thoughts home movies and music at night. But on the old good hacker time, was that hacking that was worth the word! At the time when you really got to work to get into a system. Not like today, then there are many illegal tools online to download. Tools that I could develop if I should be able to get into different systems. With the knowledge I have today and with the modern and sophisticated programs that are available! Had I been an extreme social danger since I could do a lot of damage in different systems. But back to the right time again ...

Getting in unnoticed is easier said than done. I simply had to enter a file in the user's computer, thus finding out some information that would make this infringement possible! By creating a virus or a form of Trojan horse. A Trojan horse is in many cases a real nuisance to get into his computer. To describe this little bush, you can say! That the hacker programmed into this file is activated by different commands from the user itself. At the same time, I did not want this user to suspect any maladmin istration in this file. (virus) to create simple activation commands. One classic was sending an email. When the user saw the mail and pressed to open it. If there is a sign with the text, you want to open this mail as it may contain malicious files that could damage your computer.

Of course, the user would not do this, as it was called. It was just the thing that the user would press the NO button! The no button was programmed to mean YES! But this only appeared in the source code itself. On the sign that the user saw, it was as usual. Thus, it thought the user had interrupted the opening of just the mail and it was as it looked. No mail was opened but now the virus itself was activated in the background. What the virus would do was up to the person who created the virus. Most often, it was said to find out important passwords or something else of value for the hacker.

Many hours were set to get a small program to work and at that stage, there was a lot about kicking. I was so fed up in society, so I did almost anything! So, I could feel alive. But even kicking is over, and you have to do worse things all the time to maintain that kick feeling. But when you're at the beginning of his hacker career, you'll also get crawled until you can go. Which means that no aggressive viruses could do, at first! Viruses can be divided into two categories. Aggressive and Junkvirus. In order to understand what the difference between these two viruses, one can say that aggressive viruses can erase your entire hard disk while a junk virus can only display signs that says your hair dysfunction is being eradicated.

A junk virus is harmless, but they can be extremely annoying as they can even throw up 100's of pupup's that you can get a less break on. But they can not directly harm your computer.

It would be if the junk virus is programmed to launch a massive program and the computer is in such poor condition. Maybe then? But by the way quite harmless. Like everybody else, I tried to get as aggressive viruses as possible. When I once started, there were as many as 50-70 viruses released via the internet during the month. Now there are significantly more. It is estimated to release 400-800 viruses a month now. Although it has grown so dramatically, it is only a few per year that is heard and has caused major damage. What I want to say with it! Well, it's extremely difficult to create a virus that traverses all security systems, which in turn creates major damage.

Although I knew it was extremely difficult with these viruses, I never said as never before, I do not know if it was just the high drive on me? There were long times between Annas and my separation and my progress in data. But clearly there was the driving force from the hatred that drives me.
I started doing things within a closed nerd circuit, which created a lot of rumors. People in my presence, as well as they were in the same destructive industry! Saw I made cool stuff. Being able to get into someone else's computer was at that time heavy things and the more Internet developed, the more network was on the menu. It was almost Christmas Eve every day when the Internet was just the child!

Chapter 9

As soon as I became skilled, on the field! Becoming the different orders became more and more. There was no market for just Virus. Not in this country! But to open up different layers that were online, the greater the demand for. I wanted to get a name on that market and there was only one way to get it. Do a good job! A good job was to find out where the things were. For example, in any port. What container these goods were in. Then you would have to fix shipping notes by making fake ones. So, before a job could be done, there was a lot of preparation at all levels. Just chances were no alternative when you got the duty or the police in the hedge. During my so-called practice year when I only learned how systems worked, there were many misses I did. Which I greatly benefited from working in a sharp position! When I was in a sharp position, there was no room for these mistakes! I worked to not be visible, so that I could work in peace and quiet.

Working in a hacked system usually means you only have a few minutes on you! To plant any viruses in that system. A few minutes could be a clean holiday. Usually it was very sweaty. I always had to have a second plan, if you needed or happened to put my footprints in their system. Of course, I always put an impression as we are in the digital world and touch us. But the question was just what impressions one would put there. In order to explain easily to you who are not so familiar with data, I will explain here a little more comprehensively.

All computers have an IP number and an IP number is equivalent to a person's social security number. DNS is the name of a computer server. That's the equivalent of a person's name. Then the computer also has a unique MAC no. Macnr is the equivalent of a human DNA. Much more, you do not need to explain, to understand the following.

When you interfere with someone else's data or in a network that includes multiple computers, you leave a print on their system.

The track you always leave is your computer's IPnr. The IP address can be tracked. But to avoid this ipnr leaving traces that directly lead to you, many people use a fake Ipnr. Which means that the IPN which becomes the footprint itself will then lead to a completely different computer and to a different country, wherever you are. How to do this is no direct secret. But I can tell in this book what the most common one is doing.

You simply use a smaller program that manipulates your computer's IP address. By using this program, your computer runs on the Internet via another computer. In trade languages, such a server is called Proxy server. In practice, it is quite simple. You simply browse through another computer's identity. Once you have infringed other people's systems by this means, it is very important that you use such a proxy server located in a country that does not cooperate with this country. For authorities should manage to track this proxy server, they may request, from which country and which IP number it is in this server. So, what the real IP is. Your computer's social security number! It is therefore extremely important to carefully choose which proxy server you are using. Then this can be absolutely crucial at the end. Do you choose a country that is not Releasing your information, you can do some fun things, but keep in mind! That this way is not the most ultimate. However, when you have this as a job, you need to do better infringement than the above example shows when you work with control and not with confidence. There are, as mentioned, some basic rules that all hackers work with. Of course, one is not to be discovered. Being discovered is almost always, but where it leads is a completely different matter.

But before I tell why you chatter someone else's computers in the next way. I would also like to explain to everyone who is reading this book, why this happens! Perhaps I have a desire to contribute something for prevention. The problem in the hacking world is widely known! What's more frustrating! Is that many people who use broadband today have also heard of this problem. It has also been raised via mass media through some short information.

It's about Bredbands router that you all have, as now, more have broadband instead of a traditional phone modem. The market sells these advanced routers. The one better than the other, and with a lot of features like ordinary people do not have the slightest idea of what these different features should be! Which creates a big public danger then these people and, not least, for their information as their computers store! The fact that these routers are getting better all the time is no doubt. But with new technology, ordinary people should also be warned in a more clear way. Manufacturers assume that it's only to plug in their Router, so it's ready! Quick and easy. Personally, I would like to say scary! As a customer, just insert that router to be able to share the Internet to more computers in your home.

Do you expose all your computers to great danger! You have then installed a router that is in what is called factory mode or in the default language. When your router is in that state, it means that usernames and passwords are the same on all routers from that manufacturer. Do you start to see where I want to come?

Many also use wireless networks. Wireless supports most new routers today. Which poses an even greater threat when your router is in factory mode. Some manufacturers have disabled just the wireless feature when the router is in factory mode. But many surfers today wirelessly and enable this feature. What you as a customer then suddenly have! Is an unprotected wireless network, what many people do not take on any greater seriousness. Their most common comments were! That they may like to hack my computer, I have nothing in it anyway. No, they may not have any important information in the computer, as they would miss if it disappeared! But if they knew they could be suspected of an unlawful intrusion in a bank, Am I, however, convinced that they had changed their mind set. Exactly right now! As you read this book, your computer may be guilty of a lot of different crimes. Crime you are not aware of. The worst thing is that you do not notice anything. If you are lucky, the hacker is skilled and maybe even protects you. But probably not.

How is this going? Well, you're using a different computer of course when you go out. But unlike you are sitting with a laptop. Then you are looking for a wireless network. Important is that the laptop you are using must be a so-called clean computer. Which means that Windows operating system should not be registered with anyone or something that may derive from you.

But more importantly, you do not have a file or anything that could derive from you personally.

Once you've met these basic parts, you need to find a secure proxy server to safely browse. By utilizing a wireless network, like any other person is owner of! Do you direct the suspicions directly to this person. So you're hacking on someone else's network and inside the network, you start surfing through this person's computer! So you now have a proxy server to manipulate your computer IPnr (personal computer) When you browse through the other person's computer, it means that you use it as a host computer. Already now you have a reasonable protection. But as I said! You do not work on trust but with control. Through this host computer you will be logged in for at least 3 computers. When this is done, it is time to make the attack against the exposed target. Just to make this a little exciting and interesting, I will tell you below about a complete attack against a larger company.

The company had big economic muscles and the most banal thing about this company was that they were doing IT operations. But the greater the challenge to get in. But honestly, it was no a bigjob. At the same time, I do not want to say that it was easy either. But everything is easier when you can do it regardless of industry.

We had done months of investigation at the company. By making different requests for the company's various products, we tested both filling in their web forms and sending us regular mail to the company. I soon discovered that their web forms were anything but secure, as many had serious security shortcomings.

These vulnerabilities made it possible to control where the request was to land.

However, controlling their entire questionnaire should easily be noted. Then I simply create a copy of all their mail from these questionnaires.

Which could not be noted if they did not go into the mail server statistics. Then, they could see that there had been, a lot of mail based on their mail server. But they do not seem to do this, as we could continue to collect the mail. What could we then reasonably get from this information? As I said before, the key to success is accuracy and control. In the same second you think of the word trust in this mode, you are driven. Simply smoked and you can then realize that you are in the wrong industry. Confidence is a word that you have no success with in this industry. Another common mistake many make or suffer from is Greed! By making all the major interventions in their business, the greater the risk of being discovered. One should focus on taking some, but by many different companies instead. But to sit with a company's dollars by controlling them via your own keyboard to the desired destination, seems almost unreal. There is much more basic work required before you can do this at all. But we will come to it later.

Through different dialogues with the company, we were able to provide key people who were able to sit on important passwords and usernames that could be helpful. But to discuss with a company that you should empty of dollars and other valuables, requires a certain act of talent. I did not want to raise a suspicion at the company. However, by helping us with the company, we were able to find those people who handled web pages and servers. But how do you do that? Yes! Simply open up for a dialogue. But many may wonder now, how to credibly initia

te such a discussion. Yes! You go through the company's web page to find everything from spelling mistakes on their side or other malfunctions. These possible mistakes are companies very grateful for their finding. Then the web pages constitute the company's face outward towards the customers. A serious company does not want malfunction on the website. Also a lot of spelling mistakes on such a side gives a less serious impression on a customer. It could be perceived as not the staff, or the company can spell. And the fact is that a company is not stronger than the weakest link. By sending mail to the company about these errors, we came to the right person within the company. I sent completely aware mail to the wrong person, at the company about just this error or problem. The reason for this was that the staff, for example, worked with customer service could not do what was applicable to the webpage! But thank you so much for being helpful by making them aware of the error. And they refer to the right person. I simply got the name of the right person, but it was often that they also send with the person's e-mail address in the information mail.

For customer service, it was only a normal matter to answer the customer who sent the mail. But not for me! By responding from the different people, I could divide them into the different networks, and in which working group they belonged. That way, I could easily isolate those people who were important. Many large companies have a support department. But that does not mean they are in the same local or even the same place. Thus, this isolation was important as I could easily attack the right person's computer.

This industry is not known for giving a second chance! If you failed. No! It was quite simple rules that applied in that area. I would simply just IN & OUT! So that way, it was quite straightforward.

When I planned the different networks and connected IPnr with their respective computers, I started with the next step. I had to start by checking if all of these IPs were active by sending out a call on their IP. In professional language, it is called PINGAR a computer or rather an IPnr. Indeed, all computers in the network are protected by a lot of routers and firewalls. When you send out calls to these firewalls, it will be interrupted. What is included from the beginning! But through different programs you get the kind of firewall that you fight against and can start work to break the firewall! Breaking a firewall is like playing a lottery. You never know how long it takes before you get a dividend. Then it's a program process that will let all these combinations as it can be. During the course of the rallies, one looks at working with preparing how and where to send these liquid assets or other capital goods. But a basic rule you NEVER get thumbs on! Is to figure in the slightest way, whether it's almost harmless. Control is advisable!

Chapter 10

When directing the things, you added, it must be sent or deposited in bank accounts in countries that do not provide information to Sweden in any way! When you are active in this industry you already have a lot of foreign companies. Companies that do not have the Swedish state have the slightest chance to reach the team's arm. Inserting it in Sweden would be an invalid job. Even if you do not put it on any account that would lead to you personally! So, it has to lead to someone who, in turn, has to take out the money. And then you have what you call a weak link! That's why it's not a good way to go all the time and worry about when that person should leak (Gola) information. There could also be pressure from that person that he or she wanted a bigger piece of cake. If they did not get a bigger portion of the cake, then such a person could leak, just to get stuck. Greed is a dangerous disease I have never negotiated with. But trolling out big sums is associated with big problems and a lot of work. Many used a goalkeeper to get the money out. A goalkeeper is a person who sets up with a bank account and takes the bang when the police came. This made them a lot of money. Usually for a sketch, most goalkeepers put on the A-team bench on the city. Then they had food and lodging during the winter, and they were also paid for it.

Personally, I was so scared of what happened earlier in my life, which meant I did not trust anyone. Not even on my own mirror image, it could be buggy. I made small applications (small programs) that would open up different fictional credit cards. Creating a credit card takes about 10-15 seconds and then it is fully useful.

You can then trade it over the internet without the slightest problem. Making a credit card was less difficult than knowing where to send the dollars. Quite pathetic because many people do not know how to replenish their accounts. But as I always said throughout my active time as a criminal, the problem was not how to get the money. No! It was rather how to send them and how to safely keep them without getting an invasion with authorities in the hedge. I created 20-30 different credit cards to be able to make many half-purchases. It was important that you used different credit card numbers, but it was equally important that you used different card providers. Thus, you made some cards with Visa features and some Master cards. Everything for it would look quite normal. In principle, you could use the card numbers on the maximum amounts. But why use maximum limits, then you only get an additional check from the card provider. You should not overdo it too much, as it is called wisely. Once the firewall was broken, just plant a small file to find out which URLs it was responsible personnel agreed. Once the file was in place, just retreat, just a few days later, to retrieve the file that saved the information that I would come across. Today, such viruses are called SPY PROGRAM. And that was exactly what it was. By this small program, I was able to play the file afterwards. Type as a small movie clip. The program was only meant to record the key pressures that the person did. So, it was very easy to see where they were browsing and what passwords and usernames the competent staff had. Once I had this information, the next step began.

Now you should unnoticed take control of email servers in order to eliminate possible warnings from account card companies. By creating new e-mail addresses and forwarding important mail that could make the company suspicious. When you accessed these email servers, you used to be in the first stage of the person's information last. If you know how an email server works, you also know that they usually use standard ports. Ports like 25 and 110 are so-called standard ports. But on this server, I had control of the company's e-mail to 100 percent. This step was just a preparatory step but also an extra backup if something went wrong. This check of the email would allow you to save minutes. Decisive minutes, so crucial that you always had this control. Now, you can ask the question if no credit card companies have a regular phone and could thus call and warn for these purchases so be directly illegal. Certainly, they would. But the thing is it! That responsibility for proper purchasing is shared between three different parties. Namely, the company that sells the products has obligations to be serious. Which means that the company should be clean from irregularities in order to use this service at the company that installs these stores online. The company that, opens up the webshop ensures that they secure secure online payments to the credit card companies. This usually takes many days before this is discovered. Due to the fact, that all companies want to provide the customer with simple and smart solutions, it opens up to these, fraud.

By the fact that these smart solutions are managed by computers, you can manipulate these systems. For one thing is sure! The computer is a logical machine. Is there no obstacle, perform the computer request, checking in and outgoing e-mail was a good weapon, with this check, you could easily delete all e-mail accounts, which had made it even more difficult for the police and the company to investigate the crime, It is proved that you as a person only read the first letters in one word.

Then the brain itself connects the word. By utilizing this manipulation, you could easily create similar e-mail addresses on your company's own domain name. Example: lars.arvidson@företagetsnamn.se then you could easily create an e-mail address that became lars.arvidsson@företagsnamnet.se or vice versa.

Should you send from webmaster@företagsnamnet.se which is a common spelling mistake. Many do not even think that two S is wrong. But even less wrong they think it's spelling correctly. webmaster@företagsnamnet.se. For fact, the important is the beginning and the end. Then they see that the mail comes from their own company's server. And that's the company's domain name. So, nothing strange.

But something that made great success was to read the chiefly responsible manager's mail. Especially the outgoing mail as the manager himself wrote. The reason was to learn that vocabulary's vocabulary since such an email from this manager could be revealed by writing the wrong kinds of sentences. Man is, as said, a common person, and unknowingly uses the same black words or sentences continuously. You develop your own way of writing. The boss may suffer from stabbing problems. Then an email without spelling mistakes would be completely devastating. In particular, if the boss earlier has e-mailed the person in question that one should now use. He was opposed to the sales manager as he was most interested in gaining control. This in order to check whether any employee

with less powers would ask or simply make a sample in the system that would cause the employee to make inquiries with the sales manager if he thought that the purchase would be carried out. This approach was used most when there was talk of an invoice payment. All forms of fraud are based on manipulating in one way or another. For example, making use of human imperfections. As a human being, your brain reads at least 3-4 words in 0.25 seconds, which means that even if you would read more slowly by sounding the word, your brain would not include more information for it. Thus, a weakness of man and weaknesses is basically what fraud is based on. To provide little and good information with not complete. Should the information be complete and correct, the violation would not have been possible.

If you are just trying to pick up the gold grain in a fraud you may be exposed quite early, when people do not like when everything is too good. No! It is true that in real life, to balance and create a mix of good and bad conditions. Most people cling to the jump! When fraud is usually based on the fact, that the victim is to make some kind of financial, gain. When presenting a store, it is important to present beautiful and accurate papers. The papers should be so good that they are basically better than the original paper would be. You must be able to give the exposed person the ability to check the information himself as you present. This could be some form of bank contact or other form of references.

If you are an euprophic, you count cold on checking your data in the seams. Obviously, this is not a problem as the package you are presenting is carefully and carefully planned. When you live on this kind of work, it is extremely important that you are competent in the field, as a lack of knowledge could reveal your business. Much can be planned, but definitely not everything. Some things like direct questions from the vulnerable must always be treated in a calm and stressed manner.

You should never lose your face, no matter what kind of question it will be. No one is so good that you have answers to any questions. But even this is assumed by having response responses! You can say that I'll check it right away. It may be that you can call a foreign bank. Since you already have foreign companies, you also have a foreign bank contact. But now it's really about convincing the customer that you call the foreign bank that you say you should do. For example, you ask the customer if you can borrow their home phone to make this call. If it's okay! Then it will be expensive to make a phone call. Of course, you can make calls from their home phone. You call and ask for someone who can answer the questions that the victim may have. When you come into contact, with this banker or woman, say hi, and pronounce the banker's name loudly and clearly so the vulnerable notes the name.

The reason for this is to plant a seed and to give a serious impression! Then the exposed person gets a direct feeling that this is real. The reason you really call and use the exposed phone is to give the person the chance to press redial when leaving them. Or to them at a later date, could check their phone bill on where to call. Then they would get information confirming that I called the bank and how long the call was going on. I counted so cold that the customer called the bank and checked if the bank employee existed! So, it became a matter of course. The work in progress can be described as building a house. One starts with the ground, as it is a prerequisite for being able to succeed. But but! We will leave the case for a while a return to the company.

When you have to safely manipulate a person, you must have a foundation stone. This foundation is based on some facts and papers that the person initially obtained when the deal is presented! And those tasks will be very important. We contact the IT company to make a detailed presentation of our company and what we stood for. After leaving basic facts such as company number and company name, it was now time to give the impression that we would only buy some computer equipment for our company! And it was once declared that it was only a small investment on 30 computers and screens. Which not very many companies, just order that straight up and down! Backward psychology was about!

When a salesman hears about these quantities, they become very interested as they sellers often go on a commission salary based on how much they sell. After receiving the seller's attention, he was assigned to him information that was directly relevant to this seller. One could say it was a form of mental slide show that was short and concise. By asking for his e-mail address, you could quickly and easily send any kind of financial statements, financial charts or a slide show. By simultaneously waiting for this seller to receive mailed customer discuss how hard the market was. Then there were many competitors! Through these discussions, I realized that this seller agreed that I knew what I was talking about.

What made this seller even more interested in leaving as good a quote as possible to our company. I knew that man has extreme flaws when it comes to managing a lot of information at the same time. A person can not handle a moving slide show while receiving oral information. In order to block, this information as the seller at the same time, watched his screen! I talked about similar things with the seller in the phone.

However, the information is evidently disappeared from the person within 15-20 seconds. If you do not enter it repeatedly. The information, as you assign in two different ways at the same time. Comes first when you remember them for example! When the brain's long-term memory is activated, and the person is reminded of what has been said before. Now you may wonder why you spend so much energy on such a job. You do this in order not to go there after work. Then everything comes to the surface! Then the job will not be better than the weakest link. I did not want to expose myself to these possible problems! As for this kind of business, it's like an ECG! Want to say that it can turn quickly in the wrong direction. But with a carefully planned deal it is impossible to prove. Then the team is ready on this point! It is the prosecutor's task to prove that a crime has been committed. But with such planning it is extremely difficult for a prosecutor to prove!

A prosecutor also has his duty of objectivity to take into account, which means that the prosecutor must also take into account something in the case! Speaking to the suspect's advantage.

Once you received the quotation, just send a confirmation to the company! That we accept their quotation, and also confirm where to send the equipment. When it for the confirmation itself, you used the secretary employed by the company mail to the secretary! Where you request this disc, confirm the confirmation and then send it by fax. What was a common way to confirm an order order on! The actual signature makes your so-called secretary who does not know what's going on! He or she signs by writing your name by name. Thus, the CEO's name appears on the papers but is signed by the secretary. Then delete the mail sent to the secretary by accessing their own company's server! Thus! No order has been received from the responsible CEO to the secretary. Thus, there has been a doubt as it was apparently not the CEO who wrote the order faxed to the IT company. Then a prosecutor must prove that a crime has been committed. Or was there a misconduct or a misunderstanding? You can not prove it. Thus, a court can not judge since it is beyond doubt that a crime was committed.

Once the order order had been confirmed as above, in principle, the work was completed. When the order came to the business address, it was only to deliver it to the customer. Now it was just making the process backwards. You are getting rid of the networks that you used to host computers and where you used their identities. So, I could not be revealed! Then one's own computer never existed.

Finally, what was very important was done. You picked up the hard drive from the computer and tore it into a thousand pieces. Many people think that you could only format (empty) the hard drive a few times and that all the information that existed at those various infringements would be traceable! The state has many expensive and sophisticated programs to recover deleted data information.

But by breaking down the hard disk were It's completely risk free. Once you had broken the hard drive, just spread the parts in different places. For if you had to leave a broken disk, maybe small data fragments could be recovered! Whether there is an unlikely chance that it would happen! Then you worked with Control!

To return to the preparations you can never be too careful. Obviously, the need for control is almost sick. But that was nothing that I reflected on, then it feels like a securty. By not relying on someone, you eliminate all risks that someone will be able to reveal what is happening. For the saying that says: If a person knows, nobody knows! But if two people know, then everyone knows! By all the time, that one could never trust anyone, then life became lonely. But I watered me! Then I chose to revenge society! And all who stood in the way of this revenge! Many criminals have tried to do what I did for 15 years! But only a handful of people have succeeded. Because if they managed to make the coup! Then they went in after it. For man is a flock person who always wants to get attention in one way or another. Many times, it was this attention that they were hurting. They simply said what they were doing! To wrong people and, in turn, could not keep their mouth shut. Breaking in to others' computer systems or adding another person's cash resources! Is not it just an opened door for friendship? No! Just disgrace and reverend! But that does not matter! Then I just sat and count dollars, as it would be the dear one had!

Chapter 11

I worked in two ways at the same time! Firstly, I took total control over the exposed digital world! By controlling the flow of information, one could easily eliminate any threats like alerts from other providers. I completely controlled the Purchasing Manager's mail. At the same time, the seller was lubricated by giving a good impression. It was an extensive job to synchronize the information between salesman and his boss all the time. It was extremely interesting when you really had to put your own skills to the test several times! Then I never knew when to talk to each other. To carry out a major fraud was really, laborious. For the truth, it could be hell, anytime! If you only miss a little detail. While I always had that in mind, I would be ice cold. And I can say that!

That it was really, difficult. But fraud is like any drug. You have to take larger doses after a while, to feel high!

In my life, it became more and more sophisticated all the time, in order to be able to sense that kind of kick! I started getting a name in this industry! Then I managed well with the jobs I undertook! Which is important! You can make frogs in all jobs, but not in this!

Chapter 12

When rumors spread, more and more heavy people emerged from the criminal swamp. These people were not guys found directly under the yellow pages. It was very heavily burdened guys! And that had a greeting that was a grease on the forehead! These people were extremely unstable and most often affected by it, heavier variant. But those guys had a good job, and that meant dollars! When someone said dollars, I became as hypothetical as I would get together a lot of millions! Then I had no retaliations just rolling those pink banknotes into large quantities! Who was broken! Be absolutely irrelevant! Only the dollar came in. There was a terribly big sigh in that desire. To just make a comparison, it was like you had gone through the sahara desert, without water and when you arrived, Is there a lot of water on a table. Water you can not drink, then you might understand a bit better what suck it was in revenge and dollars! With this comparison, I try not to justify what I did in any way! I'm just saying how it was. Truth!

Like all criminally thinking people, you were looking for a status in the small world. You worked for two things. You would be recognized skillful in your area, but also that you would be angry as a person! It was very important to get respect. Now that those heavy guys had contacted me, it was even more important! I wondered what was going on? Then nobody immediately tells you what would be done! Just that it was well paid, and they did not think it would be any bigger job for me! Then they apparently already checked me up! But to me seemed extremely strange when I did not tell anyone who could feel this gang. Now, when we were going to a house that lay in a completely ordinary residential area, I was more than surprised? This was not the shady neighborhood you could imagine. In fact, a small finner area. When I entered the house, we would go out into the kitchen. Once inside the kitchen there is a man with beard in his head. He seemed shadow in a more distinctive way, I did not understand what I was doing there? But apparently this bearded man would! Have a big influence. It felt strange when this man started asking me about what knowledge I had in data. Personally, you were not directly interested in telling what you had for knowledge! Then this man had not even said his name.

It does not feel good when you did not know if it was a mess you were talking to? He could be for me anybody. I responded briefly by saying my name, to quickly ask what he's called. In this book, we call him KEJA. When he had said his name! I understood that I had landed in hell's kitchen. This KEJA was at that time Northwest Skåne's largest drug trafficker. Now I sat in that man's kitchen and had a bit of half-timbered asking for his name. Njaa! It might not be so good to be cheeky about this man. But he did not prove he felt unpleasant. Which made me answer his questions. The only thing that turns my head is that I would not be involved in any drug store. It was a market I had no knowledge of at all. When KEJA asked if I could do some work for them, it was extremely doubtful when I did not want to mix with drugs. My response was that I first wanted to know what this job consisted of? KEJA replied that he would speak with his contacts and would like to be heard again. He asked if I could give him my mobile number? What I Gave Him Sorry!

He would wonder if this job was not the case, he did not tell me about. Just when we went, KEJA's son came in to eat. When he takes out the cornflakes package, the boy finds something different from cornflakes. Indeed, KEJA had put down fires that are used to blast explosives with. KEJA shouted at the guy that he would give a fan in this package! You got a little leak in the trolleys, right now one had forgotten something to be forgotten! I did not know directly that they were threatening in any way. It was probably more that it felt like you were in a movie. On the way out of KEJA's house, we meet by two big guys. One guy looked like some kind of mutant and came from a acid bath. His whole face was out of this world! These two people would later prove to be KEJAS inmates. Debt collectors.

I started to understand that this could be a problem if we were to be unhappy or something wrong. I simply did not want to put myself in such a position! Now I would go from there without knowing if there would be any job or not. I did not even know what it was about. Once again, thoughts began to shine! I who was a person who wanted complete control, did not have the least control now! A very unpleasant feeling. After about a week, KEJA called me on the phone, he wanted to meet me the same day. Later in the afternoon I went home to KEJA again. He meets me and my closest friend in the door. He said we go straight so we can talk in the car. He did not feel safe talking in his own house. By KEJA constantly talking about being guarded! As the police spanned his house and intercepted his phone, he became careful! When we had started driving, KEJA said he wanted to show where we would turn. The feeling I received was that I was out on thin ice, when I only wanted to work in the digital world. But now it seemed like I would be in the physical. In the physical where you could not change identity when you needed. It was like myself, I was the hardware! Instead of the software. But what did I have for choice now? When I was in the same car as a big hater who did not immediately see a NO! As an answer! We started approaching a port. KEJA said we would stay at the fence to talk about what he would do. My friend drove the car and KEJA was also in front of him. I myself sat behind KEJA in the backseat. KEJA only spoke with me. He had previously said that he did not like my pal! Now he asks me if I could get into the terminal's computer system? I replied that, as, long as the terminal system is online, it could go, which he seemed to like. He began to talk about two different jobs, but both concerned this port. But he would not say more when my polar was in the car. Which ended me and KEJA went out of the car to continue the layout of this job! He then asked again if I really trust my pal? Definitely was my direct answer! KEJA does not like him more for that.

I would like to enter the port terminal's computer system where all containers were registered in a database and what they contained. He obviously had two different orders that he would soon inform his buyers or the like if it could be implemented. KEJA said he could only help with a truck! And that he had a contact that could possibly get seals to containers as they were always sealed! The rest he wanted me to fix so they could only go in with a container truck. Those containers that KEJA and his partners were interested in contained JEANS and the other container would contain frozen ox fillet.

More specifically, a ton of ox fillet. This ox fillet was already ordered and sold if we got rid of it from the port in a smooth way.

Moving the container with Jeans was a little easier as no trailer truck was required. But with a ton of ox fillet that was frozen we had to find such a trailer for otherwise we would soon be there with a ton of beef ox fillet. But as I said it was not my problem when KEJA had taken that bit of trucks! I had enough headache when I was, have to get into the terminal's computer system. The problem I had! Be sure to find their firewall as engineered computer's IP, which I would need to get in. There are two different types of firewalls. Either one has a real firewall that looks like a small box and is somewhere in that building, or you use a software that works just like a real firewall, but the difference is that this firewall consists of a software program. And as I told you in the beginning there is always a weakness in a software. It only applies to finding it. Unfortunately, this terminal did not have any software software that was their firewall. No, they had the hard variant! Through KEJA's contact at the port we could provide any information that would be helpful to me. But the information about their firewall would apparently give this contact to KEJA. I was doubtful if this would work. I could not see how this contact would get IPnr on their firewall. Very uncertain, it felt! Me and KEJA jumped into the car again and KEJA wanted us to drive to another address. What we unfortunately did!

My pal drove around in a block, as KEJA did not know which port the person lived in. What we did not know was that we were driving to a known address. Want to say an address that the police had eyes on often. KEJA wanted my pal to stay in order to jump off. I'm sitting in the back seat and my polar stays at the wheel. KEJA crosses the other side of the road and reaches the gate. It turns out that the door was locked. KEJA takes up his mobile phone to reach this person at the address. It will only take a few minutes and then KEJA will return to the car. KEJA jumps into the car.

Chapter 13

Now it was raging with a lot of cops. A car crosses obliquely in front of our car, then one behind and one across the parallel. KEJA screams! That´s the police drive for hell! KEJA gets half crazy when my polar gets half paralyzed by what happened. KEJA screamed that he would drive up on the sidewalk on our right side. Then it was the only side you could get past. But my polar was like the bull Ferdinand who seemed to want to stay cramped in the wheel, with the engine shut off! All this happened in 30 seconds! Before knowing it, there was a cop on my side and aiming a sharp loaded weapon against KEJA and screaming he should leave! Actually, I have to admit that I was three apples high approximately! With a sharp loaded weapon and a high nervous cop, you get easy short in the rock and fast! If you have never been involved in having a sharp loaded weapon aimed at themselves, I can tell you that all the muscles in your entire body just release and you start to shake more or less. You get around like you've been out for 40 minutes and freezes to shake teeth. Though this is pure fear and adrenaline that completely splashes in your body! KEJA opens the door, the cop asks half-screaming if we are armed, what damn question? Well we filled in three forms before and submitted a message that we had weapons! Dumbest question I had heard in a long time! Now another mess came to take me and my pal out of the car. I walked out and got to get to my suitcase. My pal saw that it would soon look like the clean war zone!

When my pal gets off the car, he takes off his big keychart from the ignition. Then he drove a finger in the keyring, so the key pin looked like a finger ring! When he got out of the car, he said that he would put his hands on the car roof. So, he had to let go of the big one key key out of his hand! But the keys would hang around your finger then! The sound that this damn keychain created created a loud metallic sound! A sound that the police behind thought was a mantle or the like. Which made it right now, there was really a lot of weapons that the police waved with. The cop that was about to make sure my pal could be shown! Had to do, to calm down their colleagues! It became a chain reaction when the cop that pulled the weapon reacted as he did. His colleagues were not late to pull their weapons either. It was the pure nightmare that you hardly thought you were in! The cop that first came to the car bends down under the back seat! There I sat and loosened with a flashlight! I see him getting out of the car, and in his, hand he holds a small aluminum jar! It does this policeman without gloves! He stands now holding this can and he has opened. There was a plastic bag in the can. In the bag there was apparently something that I would forget about! During KEJA's and our drive, I had seen this jar but did not care about it. But trust that I cared about this jar now! I just see the cop looking at the content and then turning to his colleague. I could read what he said on his lips! It was like someone stopping the world for a few seconds. The only thing I saw was his lips that shaped the word H.E.R.O.I.N! Hell! I said straight out, abandoned! Now it's running really, and it was like having a close death experience. Everything I thought about! Now I was totally upset! What in hell would I be with this person today for, Why why?!

I was so damn pissed on myself! You should never work with what you can not! Then it goes as it did now! My thoughts were just how I would get out of this shit. To bark someone there was no chance of doing. KEJA cries at me! And said we should not say a sound and that his lawyer will get us out! But the bright comfort did not feel especially safe when I knew I would soon be in interrogation. It turns out that the can contained about 12 hectares of heroin. It was less good! Because I personally was not known to the police on this occasion, I could feel that I might be able to cope with a few years! It was a really stupid thought. Drugs are the last to be mixed with, and in particular, heroin. It turns out quite soon that I would stay there when the cop had seized us. There they stood in the scene of the arrest and with some, at least, unpleasant snubbers who promised that they would make life sick for us! If we did not acknowledge our crime! I did not say a sound when I knew what would happen when you came out if you were considered a golbag! So, jaw was and was closed about this can of heroin. I had to take off my belt, shoelaces and empty the pockets on everything! Then just start to pack a plastic pillow and a blanket that smelled crazy. Because I had never been arrested, this first night was a hell of much concern for the future and if you would see their children again!

I did not sleep one minute the first night, when there was a lot happening. Not only because it was a damn life! Without even because we were first arrested, and now it was announced that the prosecutor decided to attend us. On the grounds, that existed! Which could mean 3-4 days in that cell! An uncertainty that was just untidy. Worse, I just walked and painted a lot of bad thoughts! The one worse than the other! The children were in focus all the time and how Anna would act when she found out that I was in charge, of drug offenses. Yes, it was sweaty! Early next morning, two cops will pick me up for interrogation. It was a question that was really short. The interrogator began to explain that they did not think it was my heroin but wanted me to point out KEJA as owner of that can! I said I could not do that, because I did not know who's with heroin it was! What was not a lie! They said they had secured, his fingerprints on the can, so they already knew it was his can! My question was why I would point out someone when they already knew? But I did not know anything! And could not tell. No matter if I had been hundred because it was his, I would never point him or someone else! It is and remains an unwritten law to never breeze anyone! Then I said that I could be involved in drug trafficking. This was a pure scare tactic from the cop, to be scared and tell everything like a running water. But there was something that was really wrong in the matter! But I could not figure out what it was. That the police wanted to confirm that it was KEJA's can, while they wanted to make him point out, seemed strange? But I had not slept all night! So my thoughts were like syrup in my head, combined with a great worry for the future. I told you that I wanted a lawyer if they would ask more questions. Then they decide to end the interrogation! And I thought this might be because they would fix a lawyer for me! Another mess came into the hearing room, as this would bring me back to the arrest! Then you were locked up again! And sat in this gloomy cell that I just wanted to get out of. When I lay there on the hard bench called bed, I looked at the floor, down to the right of the cell door! I wonder where it was for running in the floor?

But I got there soon! Then I had to beat a seven. I walked at the door to call the guard so I could get out of bed! But this guard was not immediately a fast person. It took over an hour before this shift came to open so I could go to sleep. But I had now made it clear to me what the gap in the floor was for! It was a last resort if the guard would not arrive on time. Then you got a nice pee floor. It also made it possible for the guards to rinse off the floor if there was a fill in the bed that spit everything down. Many new things I learned during these hours.

Suddenly a cop opens my cell door! And says I'll take him out. We go to the bench where we had to leave our things the night before. I wondered what was going on? The cop said I'd be let go. What? How could it be? The cop told me shut up! And that I would take my things to disappear from his sight. A statement this snut would not repeat, as I quickly and easily just leave the place to find a place, to take me on! Well out of the police station was everything so damn nice to see! Everything meant a lot more now, than before I entered behind bars. It was like all the people who were in town, one's best friends! I greet everything and everyone! Yes, it was a strange sense of freedom that seemed to be the worst happiness. Something like being saloon-hungry when you're as happy. I began to think about my vengeance request on society and wonder if I got this chance, to correct my destructive behavior! And I wanted to believe that this was the fate that made me a joke! What soon should some be a naive thought!

A few days later, KEJA had also been released and I began to wonder how that it went. But KEJA's lawyer had created a bad life with police and prosecutors. Where KEJA's lawyer had asked what fingerprints were on heroin in. The police had secured KEJA's fingerprints, but his lawyer requested all the fingerprints set by the customer on this can. It was the police's forensic laboratory that established the fingerprints. When the lawyer requested all fingerprints, the policeman's fingerprints would be on the can, and it became the free point in this case. When the policeman took the can from the car, he did the big mistake that he did without gloves. A mistake that KEJA's lawyer used. That made everyone who was in the car free of charge. After that, I swore never to do drugs, or to put myself in such a situation again.

Now that KEJA was free again, he wanted us to continue as usual. I felt shaky several days after and was not very interested in doing any job for KEJA. But for KEJA it was a good day to go in and out. Like changing the style of the style. But I was now more on my guard and had developed a sense of smell that could feel a cry. I saw whining over everything. But it was 99 percent in my mind when there was no cuddle near me! But three days after I was released, KEJA would meet again. We would meet in Malmö at an address. I got there waiting for KEJA to come out of a port. After a while he comes! And he had a black briefcase with him. I felt an uncomfortable feeling in my stomach. Did not feel good! Then I only thought what the bag contained. When KEJA jumped into the car, he tells us that his contacts wanted us to continue as determined with the terminal work. I wondered if we would not lay low with it for a while when we obviously had our eyes. But KEJA did not want it! And it did not feel like it was a good location to jump off. KEJA seemed extremely stressed over the terminal job. What I could not take for the moment. We just had plans at work, but nothing was decided! Yet he was so stressed just talking about it.

Chapter 14

I sat there in the car and prayed quietly that he would not talk about what was in the bag when I could almost guess what it was in it! We would like to go around a round outside Malmö. He did not release the bag for one second throughout the trip. During the journey, KEJA tells me that I would always call his lawyer! If I needed legal assistance. And it did not cost anything! He was very clear with that! He left a business card to the lawyer and said that I could now see this lawyer more like my legal contact person. He even said if he would happen something or if he would go back in! Should I always get information through this Attorney. KEJA also thanks for not Golat him when we went in last, and he said he trusted me. But I said as it was! That I did not do anything that he had to thank for. But he thought so! After our little ride I would let him go where I previously picked him up. Before we shared on us, he said! That he called me in the morning! Then I said and left the place with a little harder pressure on the gas! Then I did not want to be with this person for a long time. Thought that his way was quite alright, when he now covered the Attorney's costs.

The next day I sat the most and waited for KEJA to call so we would decide when we were to start the terminal work. Just after 13 o'clock on the day there was a call. It was KEJA's lawyer who called me to tell me that KEJA had been arrested just a few hours after I had let him go the night before! He had been arrested, with a bag of one kilo of heroin in.
But he had left a message to his attorney that he would inform me to continue with the terminal work. Which I

did not react very much over, at first! But after our conversation ended, I began to wonder how you could leave such a message to his lawyer when you got caught with a kilo of heroin. Then the terminal work should be the last thing you thought about. Probably it was the same bag that KEJA had brought into my car, which he had now been arrested. I got cold cats at the back! Imagine if I had followed the apartment! Then I was waiting for him to come out to the car! No, there was no lack of thought of that kind! It became an extreme thought activity in my head for many hours that day. At 17 o'clock in the afternoon, it rings on my door. I looked through the doorstep in the door and saw a female and a male uniformed policeman. Did not feel like you would jump down from the balcony when I had a loft. It was just open. It was a Friday! Because I would have my children later in the evening. Then it was my weekend. When I opened the door, they wanted me to accompany them to the station. My first question was! If I was arrested? No! You're just grabs right now, for suspected serious drug offenses. What the hell are you talking about? That's what we get when we get to the station! I wanted to change my glasses when I only had a pair of training pants on me. But it was barely I had to do it, but finally they agreed. When I finished, the female snout took one step further into my hall because she was going to put on my handcuffs! Should it be necessary, do I ask? Yes, that's what she said shortly! It was too embarrassing to have to go down three stairs, in the house in which you lived! With handcuffs and two cops. Seemed as the whole staircase had a meeting, just at that time. The reason for this curiosity was that the cops had put the police car off the stairs and all those aunts in the stairs wondered what was happening!

Once inside the police car, the journey went to the station for further interrogation. Now there was an old seasoned cousin who was to hear about a drug offense. Firstly, he strategically began his interrogation to showcase a number of banners as he said would contain crimes that I was suspected of. But as they could not prove! It was his way of explaining that they had been watching me for a long time. Then he started asking me if I felt a KEJA? It was hard to deny when we had just been caught a few days ago. Yes, I know him! What do you have for business in between? What was his second question! My answer was easy! We do not have any business together. Then this policeman declares that the last thing I would be now! Was to be freaky when I'm suspected of a serious drug offense that could give me 8-10 years.

For a second, I became completely silent! I knew I did not have drugs to do and wonder where they got this wrong information from that information, we have received from your pal KEJA, who had said that I was the person who owned the kilo of heroin that he had now been caught. From pure anger I flew out of that chair. And was extremely angry. Now you have to give you! Am I suspected I want a lawyer immediately, the policeman said I would sit down now or spend the night at the station? Which I had no greater desire with. I did not want to say a sound without a lawyer. The police said they had difficulty believing in KEJA's statements and even less that I would be the real owner of the kilo of heroin when I was known for completely different things. Data and eco-robbery were my main area of work! Which had made the Prosecutor extremely fond when he was told that I would have mixed up with drugs. Now I faced two important questions! Was this the truth that this policeman had told, or had KEJA not said anything? Perhaps the statement by the policeman caused them to put ants in my mind and thus I would confirm that this was KEJA's heroin. But the fact was that I did not see this kilo of heroin sometime when I meet KEJA. Perhaps it was KEJA's way of confusing the police. I was very unsure! When I asked for the Attorney that KEJA had given me a business card, And as I wanted, I would defend myself for the interrogation! Then the police say I can go for the day! But I still stand as suspicious and it might be that they call me again for a hearing.

Now I thought my KEJA problems were over but talk about fooling themselves. A few months passed and one day there was a call for a trial. KEJA's trial! Shiiiit! It was as it would never end. But I had to show myself to the trial. When I entered, there was almost no public space, except for KEJA's brother, as he was also called for this trial. His brother had met me once before, so he was familiar. His brother said it was important that I did not tell anything! Without just saying that I knew nothing! Yes, that was an extremely easy task. When I did not know any of this matter, then it was just telling the truth. There were outside's few questions the prosecutor had to me! However, most of the questions I received most went on KEJA's and my relationship. We are just friends no more. The prosecutor asks if we had business in between. But we did not have that! Then ask the district court only if I asked for compensation for lost income or driving compensation. But I did not want that when I felt happy that my part was over. The truth, however, was another. KEJA's brother was doing the business now and he wanted me to continue with the terminal job. No chance I said directly!

Then this brother says that KEJA had done a stupid thing while he was outside. According to the brother, he had bought the kilogram of heroin on credit from those business contacts that would take against the containers containing Jeans and a ton of ox fillet. But that's not my problem I said! Who had only spoken with KEJA about these shops, the brother then informed me that KEJA had been talking to these guys and told him he had a guy who could easily get into the terminal system, now it started to be unpleasant at least!

How could KEJA have done such a stupid thing, taking a credit with these guys was less clever. In fact, KEJA and the accrued heroine were based on entering into a computer system and through these containers, KEJA's debt to these guys would be paid. But now the problem was that both KEJA and heroinet were in state ownership and well locked. Suddenly it was as if all pressure came upon me to solve these problems! Now it was anything but fun. Suddenly, it was not the question of whether or not to enter the system. Now it would only be done! KEJA's brother said I would meet a representative from these guys. Nothing i was so damn hot. Then I knew that you were more or less forced to do the job and these guys would have a face on one. Which one in the digital world did everything to avoid! But the press was almost unbearable when I started to realize that I was facing an extremely risky job. A job I did not want! The day after the trial, this representative would come to leave more instructions. The person who spoke Swedish and had a black leather jacket. He was very nice and very objective. He had a calm approach. He asked some questions if I was still interested in the job. The first thought I got was! That KEJA's brother had obviously lied to me!

He had told me that there was no return when you could not say no to those guys and that it was directly unhealthy to do that ... But the man who came asks if I want and did not have the least claim to me about it worked! What was I missing now? Something definitely did not match when I suddenly had two versions. I told that man that I would return with a message. Which he thought was okay! The representative traveled to go. When he had gone! Was I really angry with KEJA's brother and demanded a damn good explanation! He sat quietly and just staring at me as he had seen a ghost. Finally, he said that his brother had received a letter from these guys through his lawyer. His brother receives this letter which he had in turn received from KEJA's Attorney. The letter merely stated that the debt would be regulated, otherwise they would make sure he was picked up on the pitcher. More was not! But KEJA was obviously very scared when he did his utmost to stay in the detention where he was now sitting and waking up his judgment. He would thus avoid the cow in the longest! He must really trust me when I was his only resort. His brother was suddenly very humble to me, even when he was worried about his brother who borrowed a bigger sum of money to buy a kilo of heroin. An anxiety that was really justified. But where did I stand in this misery? I had my hatred and my vengeance request that would serve those big slings and would have been a little sensible at this time! I had good turned my back to and gone from there. But unfortunately, the demand for dollars and the challenge were too great to abstain. Which made me thank these guys. A new meeting was booked, where I said what I had for compensation if it succeeded. But also, what information I needed to get into the terminal system.

KEJAS's contact at the terminal now allowed his brother to handle and the trucks offered the other guys to fix. Now there was a lot of work to do. I wanted 200,000kr when the job was finished. A price that was clean for cheap, which was not the least problem to get through. They probably thought I was a bit stupid then I requested so little. But it felt like a good sum then. Meanwhile, as KEJA's brother arranged the information I needed, I checked who was responsible for the collection of these containers. By making simple calls, you found out very valuable information. When I gathered the information that was relevant to know, I started looking for host computers. Those host computers that would cover my computer's identity. But I was looking for a suitable proxy server. A server that would be far from this country. But it was also important that this proxy server did not bark out. So that you simply did not lose contact with this proxy server.

Then I through that server had contact with the different hosts. Then it would appear that these host computers attack the terminal computer. I had even said that I wanted to get in paper! Such as shipping notes and other papers that were directly necessary for carrying out this business. Unlike other hacker jobs, I would not take anything from this terminal. What I would do was to find out what supplies were interesting to us when the goods were special. Jeans and Ox fillet more difficult it was not! I just wanted to find out where these items were and what container they were in. Then I would also make a fake paper on shipping notes and signatures.
KEJA's brother would also take care of the plombering needed to make the situation look normal. The hook was to bring in a so-called empty container without waking too much interest. But especially! Why it should enter the

port terminal without a lot of questions. Through all the phone calls I called, I could ascertain who was responsible for the release that day. Then it was just making fake paper that looked better than the real ones. That probably took the most time. Through the contact that KEJA had at the terminal, his brother got a seal, with the pliers needed to seal the container. Then a stamp confirming that it was printed in from the terminal, office.

Now the job started to find their firewall. I started scanning their system through different programs to really check if they got any contact with their utmost protection. When I scanned and found this firewall, it was time, to sent a signal (Pinga) to see if this firewall responded. Which it did! Now it was time to start the running process that would break this firewall with a lot of different combinations. As you already know, this may take some time to do. Throughout the time I had contact with the customers! As if they were at least interested in how it went. But getting into the terminal's firewall began to take on the forces. However, not physically but the more psychologically. Much was the pressure I was wearing to fix this! Then a failure could have devastating consequences for a person I barely felt. But still wanted to help! Perhaps it was my own suction that pulled the most, but today I wonder if my conscience had not disappeared completely at this time. For something within me, I want to help him, though it was purely criminal what was going on. I always protected myself, thinking that it was for someone else's life, like I did this! When I knew at the same time, I denied the truth to myself.

It took over eighteen hours to break the firewall, which was not extremely long, but considering what was being done it was very frustrating to have to wait for these eighteen hours. Now it was time to get into their database as well as it was password protected. But it was not particularly difficult, it took less than an hour. When I was inside the system, I was had to enter a new IPnr so their firewall would accept our computer. Otherwise I would get hack every time you entered and there was no time for it. I simply put the host's IP code as an exception to the firewall. Which means that firewall will stop all interference from other IP addresses. That way, their firewall would not log our small visits as a direct intrusion! Then our IP number was now more accepted in the firewall. Now I would quickly try to get a picture of which deliveries could be most appropriate when the order was very specific. Clothes were no problem to find. But often these containers contained piece of goods that were spelled inside the terminal. But whoever seeks finds! And whoever has found has been looking! It is not difficult! Now, it was just finding a neat solution. Then we had to make it look like, nothing was taken from the place and how do you do that? Firstly, those who ordered the delivery wanted us to solve it when they ordered the trucks, the idea was that KEJA's brother and I would break that nose. It turns out quite soon that his brother was anything but in the planning stage when he was upset! And he said I would come to the solution. I was sadly tired of this human type. What fan would I solve? I did not deal with containers and such crap, I just wanted to do transactions of different kinds. But now I would suddenly solve this, for me hard cases. How to get such solutions when I barely knew how a container was designed. I had no choice but to retrieve, information via the Internet! Then

I'm a perfectionist who refuses to leave things to chance. But solving a problem that is to be solved on the site makes it difficult! Then it is almost impossible to make it theoretically theoretical. After a few days of investigation, I thought we would introduce the container that would be empty, filled with a number SJ pallets normally used to load pieceware. This would be introduced as an empty container! It meant purely practical that this container would be placed in a different location than those that were to be delivered. There would be a distance between these containers which became extremely difficult to handle. Thus, an entry of an empty container would not solve our problems. No, we obviously needed a smarter plan. It is strange to humans, when exposed to stress. It's like the brain locks and one can hardly find the least simple plan! I simply had to disconnect all the needs to think constructively! How could I manipulate those people who worked at the terminal and in the port area, that was clearly a real challenge! Many counted cold that I would break the problem. When I realized that the plan was a clean manipulation for the eye and not a physics manipulation, it became a bit easier to figure out a plan. The first thing I did was go to my old workshop where I started welding a grid. That had the same function as a doggaller in a car. If you think is such a grid that can be customized, both sideways and elevated, then you may have a picture of how this grid looked like. Through this grid we could create a picture of a fully stocked container. The grid had only one function, and it was to support if someone were to put on the boxes that were in the container. The grid would provide support that made the front of the boxes not fit.

Then the whole couch could easily be revealed. Now, the next problem was to solve! What would I write for the shipping slip that would accompany that container? As we had to get into the harbor area! But we were also forced to find a ride that could possibly drive this kind of container. I found a car park that seemed very Suitable for this. Now I created shipping notes from this company. By collecting logos from their own website, I could thus sort out a shipping slip that looked really genuine, with their own log! Now it was only to find a destination company that, according to shipping note, would take against Sweden's return journey. Which we could easily find, as there were a whole host of such companies. Now it was time to contact the buyers about which containers were available! And from which suppliers. Of self-preservation, I can not tell you which company we chose. But I can tell you that we collect what we initially decided. The customers sent two trucks from the capital down to Skåne. We could have access to these trucks for a week. Which gave us 5 days' lead in practice! We had a press of time, as those containers we would come over were supposed to be delivered to the company that ordered the goods. So, we had to carry out this work before postponed delivery date. The container we were supposed to pick up was cluttered and thus sealed! So, no one could introduce other things in it.

Chapter 15

Our client wanted to meet me before we did the job,
which we did, they ask me how I solved it practically
and they wanted me to detail in detail how I planned to
implement it. I told you I would use the leap we have
now, just in time! And for 2 days check the watchman
who watched the stuffed containers that stood in the port
area. We all agreed this! Then I wanted us to put a guy
outside the area for the next few days so that we could get
those times when the guard company came. A boring job!
But very important, since we did not want the watchman's
attention. We were now in a very careful but busy work.
There was no room for any mistakes in any way. It would
be enough for the person to check the security company's
times just miss a guard or maybe fall asleep for a few
minutes. Which would have given us all the wrong times.
It would have been all the way to the forest.
I as a person do not like to be addicted to others! But I
was now totally dependent on what these people would
do! Or maybe not do? But now it did not feel like there
was any return.

We could not do so much in the meantime as we awaited
the times the watchman had! And I was a little worried
that this security company would do random checks.
When we got the times, they turned out that they had
quite tight surveillance schedules, so you did not get
much more thoughtful. We simply had to make a decision
when we would turn.

We decided to do it between 02.30-03.20, giving us a maximum of 50 minutes to complete the job. We probably had more time, but we would keep these times. The guard company could be a bit earlier and we had not checked their times for a long time. Stupid to chance! We also decided that the download would take place early next morning! Then the risk of this job being detected was considerably smaller. Now it was time to introduce the container that we would move over the things in. We decided to do this quite late in the afternoon. This for two reasons. First of all, one person becomes tired of the evening, and is not so observant as it is in the middle of the day. But then our container did not have to stand in the harbor area and have eyes closed for a whole working day. The truck driver was one of the purchaserguy and, was minimally informed about this particular transport! What was the meaning Then we did not want this guy to behave nervously or otherwise call out unnecessary attention.

He received those fake shipping notes and then drove to the port gates, we ourselves were at a distance so we could see the truck, when our car arrives, the driver jumps off the truck to show off the paper, which would recognize this transport. Every minute was like an hour. I thought it took a bad time. Suddenly, it rings in our customer's mobile phone. It is the driver who calls and says that the paper he had could not be found and that the barcode they had now started was not on the shipping slip. I myself had entered the transport in the database. But what was the barcode? I turned to KEJA's brother and wondered what the hell he could miss this? He asserted that he had only received the kind of freight bills from their contact from the terminal. How the hell can he give us the wrong paper! Has he paid to ask our client KEJA's brother? His answers that he paid him fully, by paying he,1500 kr, for the job, he would get 20000 kr for that job? Said our customer to KEJA's brother. As now, it was quite willing to put a bullet in his head, with pure anger! We had to call the driver to inform him that he had to turn around. Just when we called the driver, we saw him rolling into the port area. It turned out that this barcode system was only tested and the person in the gap had said that there were many shipments this system could not find! Then they only tested the system. Then my theory became once more confirmed current greed. Due to the fact that KEJA's brother only paid 1500 kr, for the job. Did not that contact make a good job. Had he received his, 20000 kr, this would never have happened.

It was totally unnecessary when it all made nervous and create a stress that is not appropriate to have on such assignments. But it was a later problem that they found out themselves.

Now what to wait for the driver to hear and tell where the container stood. But they were placed after delivery date, which did not directly speak to our advantage, as our container would be delivered the next day. But the container we were going to empty was the first delivery on several days later. This could lead us to run in between these containers and at worst with a long distance. The driver called again! To tell us what location our container was on. Now it was just going to a place where I could connect myself to the network, for later checking out the location. I could see that there were a lot of jumping, as these containers did not stand in the same row. At this space we had to be 5 people at least. But only 4 people could run all the time, when a person had to focus on the sealing and stowage of the boxes.

It also meant that we needed 4 sackcars for easier moving the boxes with jeans! We did not know how big the boxes were. We also needed a person who could send out, so the security guard would not surprise us when we carried these boxes.

Now it was time to go down to the harbor to get over the fence. A fence consisting of three rows of barbed wire at the top. We threw up a blanket on the barbed wire so we could easily take it over us. The person who would keep track of the guarding company (Tre Lingon) would not be in the area so he helped get us across the fence. We had some that were going over the fence, not least these 4 bagpets that weighed a lot. Even though they were not directly heavy, they were not directly practical to get over a fence. Then we had the grid that was going over. It was much easier when it was possible to collapse. Once inside the area with all the equipment, just go to the container which was numbered, making it very easy to find. Before we started the job, we had to put up some kind of plan! On how we would work. Then we knew how far the distance between these containers was. KEJA's brother would handle the sealing of the container but also the stowage of the boxes.

I felt no greater confidence in his brother when I did not think he could peel up his own hedge if he put a searcher there. But even because he seemed fluffy.

We made a final check with the person who would check the security company, so nothing would go wrong. But it was quiet on that front. Now we started opening the container that would be drained on jeans, but for me it was also an extra check, so I did not get the wrong information on the content. When we got into the container, I just had to check the contents of the boxes. Well then! It was jeans just as planned. It was the brand's jeans and it was a damn mass of them.

At first estimation, we guess 2000 pairs of jeans. But we had no special look. It was simply insignificant right now. Now I developed the grid I made, in order to prepare the set. The others started loading boxes on the sackcars to start rolling them over to our container. Now there were three carts rolling all the time. KEJA's brother stabbed as fast as he could. He had to do, then we at last 4 people were loading and rolling boxes. It was full speed all the time. We really had to do, then we only had 50 minutes on us. I could not put the grid from the container empty. Then I had to let some boxes come back to this container and a 30's of jeans, which would cover up the crime. Which meant they had to empty a number of drawers in our container! So, we could set up a visibly packed container, with these empty boxes. When the last box was transferred to our container, we dropped all the baggage carts at the bottom of the emptied container. We could not bear them again. We start installing the grid and then two lines with almost empty drawers. We packed the boxes full of plastic and at the top lay a number of jeans. Which gave an impression that the boxes were full, if someone opened the container, at a check.

But the perfect crime can not be found! Which was not this either. Then we forgot two things! We had no tape for those sack boxes! Then we did not have a new padlock for the container. Then we cut it up as before. But we put on the seal, which would indicate that the container had not been opened. Just hoping they would see it as a mistake and that they themselves put a new lock. But now we had time for time and had to go back! We contact the person who checked the guards and said he would pick us up.

Meanwhile we took over the fence again! Which was less simple! For the last person in view of the threads. There was a jacket for hell, but we could afford that.

Now we left the port area to sleep a few hours before the container was picked up by our driver in the morning again. Now it was once again that you should be trusted as a safe! Then this driver would enter the port area to pick up our container. But this time it went really smoothly. It took only a few minutes and then he was on his way in after the container. It felt very wonderful. But I did not dare to make any big jumps when we did not get the boat in the harbor. As you usually say! The driver was even going out through the gates! We followed the course of events at a distance. He was now putting the hook in place, which would pull the container on the truck. Slowly but surely the container slipped up. Patience patience! I was as hyperactive as a New Year's racket. And I just wanted to see the truck outside these gates once and for all.

It was extremely exciting, though I knew that good work was done. But something unforeseen could happen! Something I had missed in all stress! I thought about everything over and over again! So, I could anticipate any problems. We talk about minutes as all these thoughts came on! And that created an inner stress with me! The customer seemed to be quite calm. Once the truck rolled out, it was like the customer blew the cigarette smoke in a hurry. It looked like he had kept the breath all the time and now when the truck rolled out, he blew out the smoke! Yes, even routine guys like the client could be nervous. Everybody excited and it looked like five guys standing at an electric fence, as we jumped out of joy! I could hardly get a whole word when we spoke to each other with pure happiness!

The driver was informed of where to put the container. We had a place down in Ystad with an old blacksmith. He had a lot of scrap on his farm, so this container would not attract much attention. When the driver left the container, the next job began to pack the boxes again. We had the trailer in which the boxes were loaded. When that job was done, we started cutting container with cutting torch. It was a bad job, but it worked well. The little pieces that the container consisted of could easily be hidden on the spot, and thus the problem was solved! The trailer pulled the goods to the capital where there were already many shopkeepers who wanted to buy these cheap designer jeans. When we checked out the number of jeans there were almost 2500 pairs. This kind of jeans cost about 500-600 kr in the store. Which amounted to a value of approximately 1250000 kr.

But the customer had to take a lower price. A price of 295 kr the pair for these jeans. You can guess if there was a huge demand for this stock. I received my 200000 kr as promised. The customer made the bigger the profit. Then 295 kr times 2500 pairs, will be a nice little sum of 737500 kr. Not a totally wrong amount. However, the customer had a few more mouths to measure.

KEJA's brother had to be glad that they did not put a bullet in his forehead. Then, through his greed, he was destroying the whole coup. After all, he had to keep 18500 kr, as he recruited, which was inside the terminal. But I learned once more! Never trust anyone! So, you will lose both a lot of trouble and to be disappointed.

Chapter 16

KEJA could now puff out when the first part of their order was completed. Now, in some way, we would find some stock that we could pick out a ton of frozen beef fillet on. But I was not so pretty. Secondly, I had a devious training pain when we moved all these boxes with jeans twice.

So a ton of ox fillet was not immediately enticing! The customer had gained a lot of confidence in me when I managed with this coup, and he wanted me to plan this delivery. But as I said! My interest in planning this was extremely low. He said that after this delivery we could make big but simple bumps! Because he had very good contacts with business owners and restaurants. It does not matter what we came across! Only there were large quantities, he sold it without any problems. But not even that made me more motivated, when I was tired and less, to have some people in my environment that were directly dangerous to all of us. Then I thought of KEJA's brother. I told the client that I did not want to work with KEJA's brother. The client did not like the brother as he could endanger everything. The problem was KEJA's debt for the heroine and was not paid for. The customer I had contact with was not the highest in the league. But he obviously had important contacts. I began to wonder who I really work for? I asked the question to the customer. But that was not exactly a question he'd thought to answer! He will answer you enough for more information. I said he could forget that question! But he only repeats his previous reply! In time…

I did not like this feeling! When talking about the feeling, it is a very difficult thing to explain. But have you ever been in a situation of a situation that felt uncomfortable, it's probably the closest I can describe it, but if you are a criminal, this feeling is extremely developed! Many times, this feeling is the only thing you have to go on. In the criminal world, it is often said that ONE WALKS ON HIS VIBES. That was exactly what I felt! I got bad vibes when I got this answer. The fixed answer was clear, so the question was more, what was not clear! Felt like there was someone form of subtitle in the reply.

Type to not ask what you do not want to know!
I could quite easily figure out that the Customer I had contact with had its head that ruled him to one hundred percent. But who were they? But to think about it would just do a noisy and now I would primarily make a decision about their offer. The client offered me the same compensation for this job. Being able to earn 400,000kr in a few weeks was not badly paid directly. Which meant that my answer was quite given. But even if the answer was given, there was no solution to where you found a ton of frozen Oxfilé equally given!

The brain cells were extremely working right now. Much thought went on to consider whether this would be a blow. Quite logically, you are wondering who can take 2,500 pairs of jeans and get them sold quickly. And then order a ton of ox fillet? Hm! Even though they did not sell all the jeans yet, I had actually been paid. But jeans are no fresh goods, and can last forever, without becoming old.

There was no doubt that this customer had contacts when they ordered all this meat. Evidently, they had arranged trucks without any problems.

Normally in the criminal world it's 90 percent bullshit! You met people who could arrange everything. When the facts were that they were completely unable to fix anything! They had some local-based contacts in the area they were active on. But usually it was no more than empty words. Many would impress to gain status and respect. But when it came to the chalk, it was just crazy! Because there was so much dirt, it was not without doubt, when someone ordered a ton of ox fillet, which was actually needed to be sold quite immediately. But it was not a sale that turned to old aunts and others, individuals. No! We are talking about buyers with large wallets and with large storage space. So, there was a lot of things to do with such a delivery. Though this did not seem to concern the customer. I was doubtful if I would fix this! But at the same time felt wrong not even trying. A little annoying when I got jobs that were not direct data jobs! Although this job might be in need of such knowledge. But such a job! Built most about moving physical goods. I honestly had no idea where I would even start looking. That some truck haulage would go around with a ton of ox fillet was unlikely. We had a trailer with a cooling unit. So far everything was good. Now we would just have something to fill it with. The customer would have it done as soon as possible. And so, it is! One must slip while the iron is hot. Taking containers and similar things makes the police begin to monitor such areas as are unattended in the usual cases. Especially if they think it's a league that's on the move. Even if you expect to get the snout hacked, you should take it safe before it's insecure. Probably it was the order of thought, and for that reason he now tried, in a little nicer way, to speed up the process.

So, it was just starting with the investigations. I did not know if you would cry or laugh, the whole layout was like a bad Hollywood script that had been tampered with because it was so bad! I felt a truck driver who was a bit half-criminal. He had done some little things for a while! But he now had more family and a wife that held him in his neck. But one could ask him if he had any contacts with drivers who drove a car. But to ask such questions! Would he at least be surprised and perhaps unhealthily curious! Then he should start searching for suitable items. I did not want him to hurt himself. Money easily makes people do stupid things. The risk that existed was that this truck driver I now contacted would talk too much! This would mean that he had permanent problems for the rest of his life. Something I would not want on my conscience! Yes! Maybe that was taking! Conscience I did not! But I did not want him to happen. It was not really a good idea to contact him when he had a family. But it is easy to say it now afterwards. We call this driver in this book Tompa.

This Tompa will begin its investigations promptly by making calls. After the first call, I had to explain to him that he got tight, since you can not talk about it over the phone. He had to start appointing times with different people and managing the gap between four eyes. He seemed to think he could talk anyway. But after speaking, more plainly with him, he realized that they were big things and wrong people to be fooled with! Tompa had the same questions I had! Who will have the things, who do you work for? Thus, questions that were natural to ask. Questions that it was equally natural to not answer. Tompa also wanted to know what he would earn on this! Whatever he would ask, that compensation would only hit my wallet! Then I was hiring Tompa. I told Tompa that the compensation, we had to take, when we knew if it all went into lock.

Tompa did investigations for over four days! In the meantime, I would have come up with some smart solution that could fix this delivery. When Tompa told me what he had, it was not exactly what I wanted to hear! Finding so much ox fillet seemed totally impossible. The closest we could come was a delivery with different of meat. There was a lot of ox fillet, pork fillet and other meat types that were counted as delicacies.

I decided to meet with the client the same day. During the same day, Tompa would have a copy of the shipping notes that compiled the contents of this refrigerator. When I later in the evening, the customer showed these shipping notes, he looked very close to them. Then he says they're taking it! Now I just had to ask if it was not just ox fillet that they wanted? Then that was what was ordered! The customer leaned up from the sofa where he sat! And look at me and say! Now we know! That you do not want to fool us! I still do not understand what he meant by it? Why would I like to fool them, I thought! It should be clean and be a quick death. And then it was like my god grandmother always used to say! You should not bite the hand that feeds one!

The customer then said that for a long time, they themselves tried to get the amount of beef fillet, but not even the ones with their contacts could fix it. Then he says! That when KEJA had said he had fixed it! They wondered how it happened! Then they knew it was virtually impossible to get it. But due to KEJAS Heroin debt, they chose to wait and not act against KEJA. Then a violent action against KEJA would mean a total loss for them. Where not KEJA could regulate its debt. I started to understand that I had become a tray in a game. A game that basically meant that I helped both the customer and save KEJA's ass at the same time, but these were game rules that were not talked about. Believe that KEJA

112

wanted to stay on the shelter when he had unfinished business with these guys! That he was threatened was no doubt! As sure as if he were dead, if I jumped off now! The customer wanted me to arrange the transport up to the capital and from there they had their own people. As soon as the truck reached the capital, my job would be complete! I wanted to return to the planning of the transhipment itself. But the customer would not know when he only wanted to know when the truck could be in the capital. I ended up going home to Tompa to sew the bag together. Just when I was about to go, the customer is ready for a plastic bag. An ordinary box that you get in the store when shopping for food. He stretches it toward me, saying that I have now been paid for the job! I look down in the bag and look to my surprise that there are lots of money in different denominations. The buyer says they are in small denominations because it is easier for you to dispense. Then they do not light up as much as big bills. I said no! I will pay when the job is complete. Things can go wrong and then I will be refundable. The buyer tried to calm me that they would not ask me if the police were to take us. Then he said that, As I did not want to hear! The customer says we will do a lot of business in the future! With a little smile on the lips. A smile that I once only seen at the last coup. I felt how gloomy my future would look like. With a lot of must! And a Client who just apologized for being interested in these jobs. In the case of crime, can you describe this world as a giant spider web, where everyone is in touch with one another or another. Which means! That if you do too much or do bad work, it is spreading fast.

The further into the spider network, the more power you had! As you probably understand, I was far out at the edge and was in the middle of what a "Smith" had called a career and there I would get a name as previously said. I began to get more and more understanding of how everything was connected. Where this spider web was a career ladder! Where you would slowly climb closer to this center's center. It was this inner circle that all the criminals would encounter. But as few did! It was like in the real world, filled with a lot of obstacles and pitfalls. But the difference was that we were busing, please take a shortcut.

Chapter 17

I have to take care of quoting a famous business lawyer who was asked how to defend the bus when he had such nice and serious business as customers. The business lawyer then replied:

Quote: There is no big difference in bad guys business compared to those big and serious companies. The difference is just that the bad guys is in a hurry, so they do not get the booking. **Quote quote.**

Which is true! Because, we bad guys could not, afford mistakes or other reasons, that could appeal to the authorities! Therefore, the companies were exempted as well as any company. Perhaps better in many areas. It would be a blameful booklet, or it was a pure genius feature. Judge yourself!
But back to work!

I drove home to Tompa to make the last plans that were required for the job to succeed! Now we had to find the weaknesses that would give us the opportunity to succeed. Tompa had found a colleague who was tired of his employer, who seemed to pay this driver too badly. For another reason, I could not see when he could put up on our plan as were the following.
I told Tompa that he would fix a number of bad glow plugs to the truck we would cut. Glow plugs are the equivalent of spark plugs in a regular car. But all the diesel engines have glow plugs. Everyone who drives a car that does not go on all cylinders knows that it's going to be bad if this error should occur.

The idea is that this driver should drive into a bigger resting place! Such places where people can stop for a coffee. But even there, drivers can stay overnight. Then we would use the same radio frequency that this canal used on its comradio.

As the driver drove into such a place, he could replace the lighted glow plugs against glow plugs that worked very badly. These glow plugs had Tompa got to the workshop where they usually used the trucks.

Meanwhile, as he replaced those glow pins, he would not listen to us. No! Instead, we waited for this driver to make a request from his employer via communication radio if there was any other driver available and could possibly take his driving? Then he had to drive to the workshop with his truck. What he really said, Where the trailer was on the spot and that he started driving to the workshop. We did not want the guy to have a problem. By calling only the yard that he drove for. At the same time, he gave us the clearance to pick up the trailer with the meat. But just to cover up the change, the story was that the driver had broken at the same time it took to replace the glow plugs. The fact that he stood still could also be certified by people around who had driven into the resting place. But the most important proof of this break was! The tachograph that all professionals have installed in dashboard! It is available for the police to check with a check so that the driver is not driving for many hours without a break. A perfect cover. Then the glow pins were bad, which could also be checked afterwards.

Tompa pick up the trailer with the meat, with the trailer carrier ordered by the customer. Then he drove it out into a wooded area, where the other trailer was empty. When he arrived, just switch over and reload. You did not want to drive around with a trailer towed. Now, this began to be astonished to bear again. We only had ordinary construction gloves to wear on our hands, where the cold quickly went through. We got very tired, then 20 people needed! Then there was a lot to wear. When we finished! Put your hands like two frozen fish sticks on a low note. I had received a phone number from the Purchaser, which I would send a text message to. Message would be completely empty, nothing written. Which tells me that the goods were heading to the capital, to the exposed location!

It would take 10 hours to reach this destination. So, one keept the speed round! You would not get the profithungy fingers of this mess. But the round took a little longer when there was a lot of road work. When the truck was over, my job was clear, and I had already received the payment! So, then it was a party when Tompa came back! It was a barbecue with lots of spirits! But for some reason, we do not grill Oxfilé!

The customer was very pleased with the job and advocated a great future cooperation. I had a good capital on my pocket. Tompa and the other driver should now get their share of the cake. Because we had not talked about it before more thorough, it became a negotiation only now. Tompa ask me what I had for the job. One question I ask would prefer to avoid answering! So I said they had to say what they wanted! Tompa had to pay his colleague what he received in payment. Tompa thought that a 25 maybe 30 thousand for both jobs was reasonable! Then it was just like I got a Flashback thinking about what KEJA's brother had done to the connector inside the terminal!

Then I would not look good if I fell for the Greed myself!
I told Tompa that he received 65000 kr for both of them.
Then I said I do not care what you give your contact! But
make sure he shut up and that he should base the amount
that was reasonable to guarantee him quiet. Now you can
never guarantee that someone is quiet! But by giving
them an amount they felt satisfied with! Did that matter
make it a little safer? I myself, as you probably already
calculated 135000 kr. But there was also a lot of work on
planning this coup. Tompa shouted her love and said she
could shop the whole weekend if she wanted to. Another
thing you absolutely should not do. Lay low! Please do
not include in his vocabulary. What now became a
problem for him! Then he promised his wife to buy the
whole weekend. Such promises can not be given to your
wife! In order not to let her shop late! No, he had
problems now. I could dare how he did with his dollars.
However, it should be noted that their family acted widely
and could lead to a lot of unnecessary problems, for me
should this Tompa come into a police interview, one
would lead to the second, and that ended with his wife
sitting in interrogation. Then it would have been run. And
you are not stronger than the weakest link.
Tompa lay on the more naive level, because he did not
think for a second that this work could be derived from
us. But to BELIEVE a lot of things belongs to the church
world! Not the criminal world! There was a lot of word
exchange between Tompa and me! Which meant that he
gained a better understanding of how important it was to
LIE LOW!

Tompa's colleague, who left the trailer at the resting
place, was briefly called a police interview to explain why
he left the goods. But his story was sustainable, and the
police could check afterwards. But where the meat took

ahead, is not yet resolved! The crime is today prerogative. Now that you have described, this crimes above my own thoughts are why you did not give up in doing more crimes for a while. When I had served on two crimes, two salary was equivalent to the time when this crime was committed. The earned amount of these crimes was 335000kr. An amount that was a lot of money at that time. But do not think I was happy about it. Had I started to be Girig myself? Probably!
I thought I was cool that could succeed with these crimes! And, as I thought, it was crazy. Yes, you hear yourself! Where was I heading? A confused soul who tried to revenge, while tending to make it illegal, legally pure mentally.

Chapter 18

I had begun to give the grudge an increasingly clear face. But there, as a person, I had put my feet down in the valley of denial.

I had asked the customer who I worked for? But now there had been quite new questions in my head that mourned. Who was myself, what did I do? All these self-directed questions had become more and more. At the same time, I denied all the mistakes and breakages that I did. I tried to rewind the tape in my head to see my own role in this misery! That just made me feel bad. But to flush back, be tied up with the band. Why could not I think of it? Was it my body that defended itself by welding it again the door to the event that I've had? It all felt strange. Why were such blockages? Then I could not think of it! It is only now that I write this book as I really see the blockage so clear. It's scary that it was so bad! Anyone who are or has been a criminal is persecuted by these questions! Sooner or later. When the questions and consolation choices appear, there are only two things to do! What you should do! Were breaking the destructive way of life and promptly request help. This would make it possible to reintegrate into society. It is the theoretical vision, which does not work in practice!

In fact, many criminals early realize that it is not a sustainable life. But you need to get professional help breaking the behavior. The community usually reacts late. Many times, society does not respond until someone is sentenced to some form of punishment. Preventive work is bad, and it will always be. Even if the authorities have become better, their efforts are like a gravel grain in the ocean. The consequences that will be! The authorities' passive absence can be similar to cutting into your finger. After a while, the wound heals, the corpse slowly shrinks, but the scar is always left. But I want to say that. If authorities wait for their preventive measures, they will be allowed to drop the buses on various penalties such as prison. But how good than prisons or care measures are! Then there will always be a human being! With a wretched personality!

I had begun to think about the role that criminal myself had. I did not belong to anyone just that occasion! But I still did a lot of work for different organizations who wanted my services. In the ordinary society, I had been seen as a resource which was linked to the wrong clientele. But during the first part of my criminal career, my mission was as a freelance worker. With the big difference that I had to constantly break the law, to be able to do my job.

In the lower world, you were like a Pointman. A Pointman is more advanced than just doing a job. No, a full-fledged Pointman could do work for different organizations, but could also afford them. But just that bit, to mediate, I was not so interested in. But it happened relatively many times that I was allowed to get between sellers and buyers. While a deal would be made up. Many times, there were heavy organizations behind the product. But the buyer could be an ordinary company, who wanted the goods. Then the organization puts in its Pointman. Where this acted as a form of conversion tool between these parties. Suddenly, one had become involved in a rather Pointman characteristic role. A role that meant that I consciously took great personal risks. Should anything go wrong, I was out on thin ice.

The police initially had extremely hard to place me. Or to which organization I belonged! What I now know, they greatly puzzled. When you play with such heavy criminal gangs, the police have quite a lot of resources available. The organized crime should be kept under surveillance. When you were in such circles, you quickly came under surveillance. I was now a step even heavier criminal. The police soon followed every single step I took. I had indeed ended up in one of the police's secretest records. That registry is called ASP and is a voltage register. Now it was not something that I received a letter in the box about! That I was introduced in this register. That's something I found out a long way after! I found out that I was entered in this registry, at a trial! There the prosecutor had written it in his arrest. That I should be detained for unlawful threats and there was a great risk that I would carry out these threats. But also, that I was a heavier criminal person and that I was in ASP. You can say that the district court approved the prosecutor's wishes by a few keywords. He said the words ASP, Mc related, unlawful threats with baseball. Then I was arrested with complete restrictions. The little damn prosecutor he was only three apples high, but he was so angry at the prison trial! So, you could think he was at least 2 meters high. He completely went to bed when he heard the word Mc club or the like. He completely loved putting me behind the lock and boom. What organization I finally belonged to, I chose not to go out with. Then it would not benefit me purely healthily. But the biggest reason is that this box's message is about me and how society acted against me. And how I personally reacted to doing extremely stupid things against companies and individuals. But back to event.

The detention would be according to the Prosecutor for a recovery that I would have done. Which I had done. I had received a new kind of mission and would drive a debt and scare the shit of a guy. Normally, there were always two in such recoveries. But it was considered a fairly simple recovery and that, as a person, I was like a maniac with a baseball tree. I did not make myself crazy at that time. It was a time I probably should have been minded. In theory, I did not have any retaliation on any level. I was going to go for this job, and it was almost 17 miles to the target. The fact that I had a job to do was the same thing that you got married to the object. That's the person you would get from the money. As long as the job was not done, where You are married to this person. Now you can wonder why you say betrothed? The word betrothed comes as most know from Engaged, but in ancient times it was called betrothed when giving a girl an engagement ring and promised her to marry her within a year. But in the lower world, this word has a completely different meaning. The word initially comes from a professional murderer who had it as income source. When they got an item, they would settle for a sum of money. But usually there were several assassins on the same object. Therefore, these professional killers were initially betrothed with the object until the job was completed! But for my part, it's about the knee bowls of the object or a crushed nostril. I was willing to go any way. It's terrible to say that! But then I would have become like a person.

Chapter 19

I had started deleting those 17 miles that lay before me.
You began to peep yourself from the first mile and until
you arrived! In the car, I had a wooded baseball tree of
the rough type. I thought the bought baseball trunks that
were on the market simply were too clever! And bent too
easily. I wanted to do a good job. When I arrived, I
looked up at the apartment in which the object lived. It
was on the gloves! And grab the baseball tree. Because I
was on this recovery myself, I even had a gun with me. A
Beretta 92F. A weapon that US military officers have as
their standard weapon. Went from the car and towards the
doorway. When I got up on the right floor, the door I was
entering was already open! I began to think that it felt like
I had bad vibes. It was lit up in the stairs where I stood.
And I did not want to pull up my weapon that I had in my
pants behind my back! Then there could be people
looking through the peephole in their doors. After a few
minutes the lamp goes off the stairs. I put the bolletree
against the stairwell wall to get my weapon and make a
mantle. Now I stood there with a sharpened weapon and a
bolletree. The adrenaline pumped on quite well! I took a
role that was not really myself. The sick and obsessive
person I had become, step into the hall and proceeded into
the family room. No one was there! I checked all
boundaries after someone who could have been the
victim's acquaintance or the like. I understood that the
person had withdrawn from his apartment, in a hurry to
save himself. I go out again, from the apartment and hear
from the apartment side of it being spoken. It was heard
as someone stood close to the door and pushed. A sound
that arises when you have a gap between the frame and
the door,

and when you press towards it becomes a noise that occurs. I quickly pulled up the door that was unlocked. Before the door stands a guy with a mobile phone and talking. He was talking to the guy I was looking for. The guy I was looking for had seen my car and then jumped into his neighbor, to quickly climb down the balconies at the back of the property. The guy in the hall more or less fall back and start crawling into his apartment! While he said, do not push me, do not shoot! He was terribly terrified. I secured my weapon and put it behind my back again. The guy started to calm down a little while he did not see my weapon anymore! I tried to explain to this guy that I was not looking for him. But even that I wanted him to tell me where my object was. I saw how scared he was! His underlips trembled with fear, though I did not in any way threaten him. But in his world! Be well this intrusion more than enough! At first, he did not know where the guy had gone! But after a certain persuasion he told. That the guy drove home to his parents. I said to that guy, you lie, you will have to look for your knee bowls the rest of your life. He clearly understood my message. I got the parents home address and gave my boy a nice evening.

Since I had no local knowledge about that city, I had to look for a gas station to get a map. When I had located the address, I drove into the parents' entrance. It was winter and some snow on the ground. On the yard it looked like a whole football team had sprung around there. The snow was trampled down almost everywhere. The house was dark, no lights shone. Just a christmas star in some of the windows. It looked like the house God forgot! Absolutely abandoned! I walked around the house to look through the windows, but all the people shone with their absence.

At first, I thought the guy did not run here at all. But all footprints that pushed down the snow in the entrance were recently made! How could they know I should come here, had the neighbor I talked to, warned these people? I became furious! And with great determination, would drive home to this neighbor again. But this time I would be very clear, so he could take the message. I was now completely convinced that this neighbor was behind this failed recovery attempt. Which meant that in criminal circles one could lose his face. Again, on the street where the neighbor lived, I now saw that this person apparently had also emigrated. Everything was black! I drove past and turned the car, so I could sit in the car and see if there was any activity in the apartments. I had not been sitting in the car for a lot of minutes when a police car was moving towards me! It was fast down with my head before they saw me! There I sat there with a sharpened weapon. In my pocket I had a handful of Stesolid 5mg. These were tablets that, in this amount, had easily become small narcotics. The policemen did not see me! Without slowly slipping past me.

The pulse increased sharply! Now it felt like I was hunting instead. I left the car! But leave the baseball tree to leave the car. I had received the tablets of my so-called friends, if I thought it was hard to make the recovery. Then a recovery can get very bloody. But as I said! Then I left the car to find a smaller alley or the like. I had to drop all the tablets in a well on the road. It was definitely the safest. When I still thought if some kids would find these tablets, it could have had serious consequences that I did not want.

When I threw the tablets I walked around the house and reached a hotel. I thought I book a room in a fake name and pay in cash, so I'll take the recovery tomorrow! When

I arrived at the front desk there were two women. It was quite late at night so you had to call a clock so the doors opened so I could come in. When I get in touch with one of the hotel staff, I ask what it cost a single room? She turns to her colleague to hear what the price was. When this one comes to tell me what the price is, I'm looking at her name plate as she had on her jacket. It was the same surname as the person I would make the collection on. This last name was very rare name, so I react immediately when I saw the name. I quickly got an apology! After she said what the price was! Then I said! Then I'll have to look further. It was simply too expensive for just one night. Thank you for me and walked out of the hotel. When I got out of the hotel I thought how small the world is. Here you run around in a city I had no knowledge of. Finding a hotel! And there is a relative of the object. Whether they knew each other or not, it was strange in any case. I called my friends at home, and their advice was to go straight away. Now I had marked what we were capable of. Which in many cases was enough.

But no! I should have got this guy! And I got to his neighbor who was the pure bonus. I started walking around the city when I waited for the return of the object. It started to get a little later in the evening and it was quite cold outside. There was a gallery with shops. I went in to buy me something to chew on. But it just ended with a piece of chocolate! When I warmed up, I walked out of the mall to continue on my car. I did not get that far from the mall, when suddenly it started to smell cop shit! Even because it was a bigger city! But now the policemen were either on transit, when it felt like the whole police force had come to that city. Or were they looking for me?

I faced that they would be after me. Prosecutors tended to fend for the smallest of them. They were looking for errors and crimes all the time. But this time it would turn out that the neighbor of the object had not only warned the object. He had also taken care of calling the police. It turned out that the guy I should have had, as I said, jumped down the back of the property and then jumped out on the road to take the registration number on the car I had come in! My registration number had the neighbor dialed in to the police to complete his notification. That's why it took such a time before the police responded. When the police got to know who I was, it took a screw! But I did not know this when I walked in the square. I tried to get away from the square. I started halfway back into the mall to get to the other side of the mall. Now I was looking for an alley again. But now it´s a hurry I can say! I had a sharpened gun on me and you did not want to get caught up. The only thing I thought! Where to find a street ground again! Then my problem would be gone. I began to glimpse a pit with grids, now I thought! And started with my left hand to search for the gun, which I felt more like it was there. The pipe was crazy when it was cold outside. I grabbed the gun and took out the magazine and made a mantle so the shot in the race would come out. The idea was to just throw it between the grid, but it turned out that the gun was simply too big! It's not easy to get a good time, if such a grid, so I could lift it up! Now it was about thinking quickly! I looked at the magazine for the gun and thought that the small heel that is located at the bottom of the magazine could help, so I got the grid! I drove a piece of magazine to get around my lap so it clung to the grid. Which it did! I raised that grid so much that it got a bit on the street side. Now I could grab the street grid. I just eased down my gun and the magazi ne. Then I felt carefully if I had something that could be directly unsuitable for a possible arrest. But now it was just my piece of chocolate left in my pocket, thank you! I started slipping around the city like a completely innocent person. But just as the criminals see cries, the cops see criminals, as sure as Amen in the church. That sounds strange! But many times, we are seeing each other in a strange way! But in this case I was since a few weeks ago wanted by the police. Which I neither knew, at this time.

When the neighbor of the object completed his registration with my car's registration number, the city's police were blowing with the big drum. The policemen, as usual, hunted the fountain and the like now had a Mc related case with a wanted person. It was pure Christmas Eve for them. Now I began to experience this city was very small and cramped. I walked around to see my car at a distance. But there was no way to retrieve it, as there were policemen at both ends on that road.

Not for that was a direct surprise. But I still did not want to accept that they were looking for me! I decided to walk around the snows, and to get a few blocks away from my car. When I arrived a few blocks from my car, I turned up another way to find out from the inner city. As I started on that road, I could now see a policecar up the left, further up on an adjoining road. Just one minute after I saw this policecar, there will also be a regular policecar down the road where I turned up. I picked up my piece of chocolate to just do something, so it would not seem strange that I went there! Then I thought! So fucking cork thought! Stupid so i'm just blushing i'm writing it. Yes Yes! The regular policecar drove quite close to me before it stopped. A cop goes off and starts shouting my name, and then it was time to realize that it was me they were after. It was a middleaged police who slowly began to

walk towards me, with a policeman behind him, with one hand on his service weapon. This policeman wanted everything to go smoothly. Did you have any weapons on you did he ask? They behaved very tense and awaiting. I replied that I was armed! Now it was really tense. You heard and saw this, police take a completely different position and voice mode! Put away the weapon, he says, with a more determined voice! I said I'm just armed with a piece of chocolate and I did not want to leave myself because there was too much left. The policeman then screams me to get rid of the weapon again. I have no weapons I told them! We do not believe that! Sit down, lay down! Your satan's psychopath. I understood that they did not appreciate mine chocolate Jokes. When I lie on the ground, there are also police officers rising from the adjoining road. It was the bugs from the bus. The whole mood had become unpleasant and tense.

They first put on the male boots on my back. But after visitation, the elderly policeman said that they were going to put the handcuffs forward. If I was calm! Felt like unnecessary energy loss to fight against! When they put me in the policecar they started driving towards the police station. We entered the back of the station and entered through a couple of gates. Once inside the garage they did not open the doorway from the gate behind us was completely closed. Before the policeman opened, he told me to keep me very calm! And made sure I did not have a chance to get from there. I then asked him what I had done? One question I have asked a number of times during the course of the journey. He just replied that I knew very well. He wondered at the same time how I could manage to scare away a whole family in just a few hours. It turned out that the entire family of the object was at the police station when they were terrified. The policeman brought me in an office room. Just after us another, police arrived who would sit and wait and check me. Meanwhile another policeman contacted the prosecutor to hear what decisions would be made in my case. The policeman on duty thought it was awesome to catch the bus from Skåne. He had a rather humble way. He asked what the bus did so far up in the country, as they were not used to having such criminals of this caliber. I did not have any longer answer but answered him that it was business! He immediately wondered who did not manage his business? That was a question that was not answered. When this, police started to understand that no answers would come from me! He changed tactics and began to talk generally about this city we were in. And what famous artists there were, who made the city famous! YAWN! Completely uninteresting! I just wanted to hear what the prosecutor had to say and what decision he or she made. It took at least an hour before they caught a prosecutor who would make a decision. They also dialed my social security number so that the prosecutor could make a decision. I knew so much that I was wanted. So, the prosecutor already had a reason to lock me in, but apparently, they would get me on several points. It was above all this new matter that they would bind me to. After a long wait, the policeman who put the handcuffs on me went into the office to announce that the prosecutor made a decision, to arrest me for grossly unlawful threats, illegal possession of weapons that would be testified by witnesses when I had no weapon when they arrested me. Then he would hold me for burglaries in two apartments as well as a righteous procedure. Without it I was already wanted because I was suspected to knife a boy hard in Skåne. So, this prosecutor had all his feet.

Chapter 20

I requested a lawyer immediately, which they would arrange for the following morning. Now it was handing in things again. Brace strap, shoelaces, earring and empty the pockets. Then it moved into the cage behind bars again. Hell, how tired I was going in and out as the worst yo-yo syndrome. But I did not have much to say about. I could only lay down and wait for the lawyer to come in the morning. After long night, finally my lawyer came around nine o'clock in the morning. It was not the lawyer we used to use. Then the lawyer would come to a later date. But I did not like a new lawyer, but it was a lawyer anyway. He began to present himself and give me a business card with his phone number. Then he told me that this was hard! There was witness according to the police who saw me with weapons and even said that I threatened this with that weapon. What was a clean lie! He had clearly understood my hearing as a threat. But I had not directed any weapon against that guy. I stopped the weapon. But he had seen the weapon so much I knew. Now the lawyer wanted us to stay low and await upcoming hearings during the day. I did not want to be heard which I clearly declare to this lawyer. He says that we make the most of answering the questions.

But I was drilled to say nothing. I had learned to answer words like that.

COMMITMENTS, BALANCES, PREVIOUSLY.

Otherwise you would shut up.

This lawyer and I obviously did not have the same opinion regarding the interrogation. But we found that I would participate physically in these interrogations. According to the law, you have the right for any time with your lawyer. But I would like to say is a modification of the truth. We were quite soon called for the first hearing after my lawyer had arrived. Now there was a new policeman who presented himself as an inspector. Nice would be! He wondered if I would ease my heart and acknowledge some crimes. My lawyer said his client denied crimes on all points. He then began to talk about my Object! Who had felt threatened by me, strange! I thought! I have not even met the guy live! The lawyer replied that his client did not even know who this person was. It was strange, said the policeman! The person who made the application has described your baseball tree very detailed. Then something even stranger was that your car was below the apartment of the object. But what the policeman thought was quite sensational was that in my car stood such a baseball tree. This was strange! The lawyer turned to me wondering if I had an answer to why I had a baseball in my car. I replied that I started playing baseball and practiced a lot to meet the ball. The lawyer and the police laughed for a short while. Did not feel like they believed in this version. I told my lawyer that a baseball tree was not illegal. The police heard what I said. No, police said it's not, if you hit balls. But in humans it becomes very illegal. My Attorney pointed out that there was nothing that his client would hit anyone with a baseball tree. Then my lawyer told me that it could be a coincidence that there was a similar baseball tree in the client's car! As the Object's neighbor had described. The policeman says that it could not be a coincidence, just when this baseball tree was home-grown, and it was the roughest baseball tree he ever seen. The baseball tree was over 12 cm in diameter at the front of the tree. The lawyer just snatched me a little and then told the policeman that there was hardly anything that violated any law. What a policeman had to admit! The policeman said he did not even see a baseball player having such a big baseball tree. He would like to explain why you had such a large baseball tree. I just had to answer him that the bought baseball balls bend easily if you hit hard! On a ball said the policeman? I'll answer that!

The policeman looked at me as he wondered if I thought he was completely dropped behind a cart! He then asks if I felt this was incorrectly perceived by the Object to feel threatened by me. What my lawyer replied, that was quite rightly understood. The policeman wanted to know what I was doing so far from home. I was free and just wanted to see me around Sweden! I answered Mr. Inspector.

The policeman wanted to finish the interrogation and explain that I could stay in the cage for a while. My lawyer said they could stay on for a few days. I told the lawyer that I knew these rules, so he could stop telling them about those rules. Back in the cage again! Now it was like all the police were running and watching who I was. A new face appeared every time the inspection door was opened in the cell door. It turned out to be of great interest to who I was. It was probably quite cool stories at the station about who took me and how it happened. Had I known about this interest, I would have taken a coin every time they looked into the cell where I was sitting. It would have been a lot of money.

I began to get pissed and rang at the clock, so the guard would come. I want to call my lawyer now! You'll have to wait, he'll come later. This was actually a misconduct! Then you have the right to contact their lawyer whenever you wish. But that's what the law says, but reality is a completely different story! You do not have much to do when you sit there in the cage, and in the arrest it hurts. Three hours after the end of the hearing, it was time for a new hearing. Mr. Inspector came by himself and opened the door to my cell. He wondered if I could think of answering questions without a lawyer. NO! not a chance!

He closed the door of the cell and pulled back the inspection door so that smoke was over. He was very annoyed by my no to the interrogation. He returned after about 45 minutes. Can you travel now? Wounded the Inspector? Your lawyer is in place, he said great irritation. I had to travel to join a hearing room. My attorney was already in the hearing room. Then we'll see the Inspector! You have, according to the claimants, threatened to shoot those knee bowls with your gun. What gun wondered my lawyer? Now the lawyer wanted to know what this was for the assertion the Inspector spoke about? What made my lawyer damned, who said they could not sit here and insinuate!

Yes, so it is! The plaintiff had left this statement. What the Inspector reported to us. This inspector had a lot to come with. But as I said! Crime was denied on all points, and it did not make me a person, more popular at that station! After many denials, once again it was time to return to the bleak cell. When you sit locked and it's quiet, you start to think about everything badly done in your days. I got a feeling of revenge. I just wanted to send up a pile of my friends, to those people who notified me. I could not call. It was only the lawyer I got in touch with. This made them because I could not complicate the investigation.

Chapter 21

It started to be late in the afternoon and now it will be an alert guard! Who worked extra on the arrest and informed me that I would go to the district court for detention! How the hell could a "fucking" guard come and say it? Then it should be my lawyer who inform me of a detention deal. When will I be in prison, I wondered? Tomorrow at 10.00! Now I was really pissed off and started out with pure rage eruptions to kick on the "fucking" bed, which was the only thing I could do. I was so angry as the guard opened the inspection door to ask me to calm down. I asked him to go to hell! And when he came in, I promised to drive the bed in the ass on him. He did not go in! But he poured on a little mood's fuel by plugging his face into the inspection hatch and saying that it was a threat to the official! He should be happy, he was on the other side of the cell door.

My Attorney arrived just before 18:00 in the evening. He apologized so much for not announcing earlier that day that there would be a detention deal. Then he says that I will probably be detained. I wondered how in hell prosecutor could go to a prison negotiation with these clever evidence and basically based on hearsay from the claiments. The lawyer says that if you move with such a clientele you can expect to be often detained in bad evidence, when I was in a register as in the police ASP register. Then I had often appeared in the police rolls. I would probably be detained on past incidents. Felt clumsy and it did not give me more faith in society when I was already so hateful about it. Now you can think I was guilty. But it is not relevant just in this matter. Society must prove to be guilty of a crime. You can not judge old incidents, then

it's wrong with the legal system!
But with the facit of my hand, I can tell that society often makes a serious overthrow by judging on the hearsay and on, people's backpacks. What is a common danger when innocent people can be convicted. Now I had been on recovery, but I had not hurt anyone. But it could have been a person who had been a past and who had begun in his life and who was accused. Would this person be arrested? The risk is great! It is completely unacceptable that it may be the case. This country has a lawbook that is clear but not enforced. Why?
In the European Commission, it is clear that one should be considered innocent until the opposite has been proved. It is also said that a great social danger has arisen, as the media repeatedly judges the suspect before the courts make a decision. At the same time as the law says we have pressure and say freedom. That politicians can not believe that these laws are violent and that there is a need for a change of law. But you do not react to the laws, from the person you personally have been exposed to. Is convinced that many now, think I feel sorry for myself! And that I, as a person, would have been unfairly treated by society. In fact, I have been a damn pig against many people in my days. Probably the word pork is too fine, since I have done a lot of illegal things. I have been called for most of my criminal time. But regardless of my bad behavior, it does not justify the fact that the society itself makes a break and locks the bus through abuse of power! Everyone is entitled to a fair trial and shall not be convicted of society before the verdict has fallen. But even if our country is to comply with the European Commission, innocent people are judged every day in our elongated country. Both in courts and in the media.

But back to action!

I did not have much to the top of this lawyer, now he or she has already reported a loss. This by believing I would be detained. I simply had a lawyer who made only the most necessary for his clients. He did not immediately have a fight. It was not without feeling quite alive for the moment. morning after, then the breakfast came in and I spoke to my lawyer a few minutes before it went to the district court for detention negotiations. Of course, I was arrested for avalanches and that there was a collision danger if I was released at this, stage. So it was just back to the arrest to await download to the Fence! The detention staff who would come to pick me up was not in a hurry to come! It was not until closer at 17 in the evening, as something began to happen. I had just had a shower twice since the arrest. So it was better to be detained, since there was a better cell and clean clothes so I could feel a bit fresher. When the staff came from the detention, there was a man and a woman. Strangely enough, it was the female guard, who would sit side about me in the backseat. Before we went to the detention truck, the policeman who interrogated me would put handcuffs on me! Handcuffs were for about 20 meters. When you're in a truck! Looks like a little cage behind the driver's seat in hard plastic. And you have to look out to the window. In front of a sitting it! A similar to a bent iron pipe that is anchored in the cage itself. This used to, bend stiff people in. When we got into the detention truck, the female crew said she was going to take care of my handcuffs, but at the same time they would be on me the same second as I was bullied in the car! She said she knew what we were saying and that we would not knock a woman down this woman would be a plit. Apparently she was read when we did not use violence against women or children. It was an unwritten law that was always complied with. We had half an hour's drive in this truck before we arrived at the detention center in a big city. Now it was in a policehouse again, then a lift up on the top level, in that building. Now it was time to register with the Central Guard where they wanted to know a lot of things like for example! If I went on any drugs or abused drugs. But I could answer no to these questions, since I have never actually taken any form of drug in my body, I mean narcotics. Of course, I drank a lot of alcohol instead, now it was time to leave all their own clothes, instead of getting clothes where KVV was on. KVV stands for the Criminal Care Agency. Then I only got a pair of sandals.

Now it was just in a new cage, to break down. Because that was it! As it really was about! But in the district court it is so called Collision fare. Wishing all prosecutors or other government officials to be seated for a few weeks. Then they would have a much more humble side against those who are locked in the prisons. For you to be aware! To be detained is far from the same as being punished by an institution! Where the interns have things to engage in! So like work and meet other interns. Thus, a more human life. Meanwhile, a life in the custody of restrictions means isolation within four walls and one hour's break per day. So you can sit in your cell 23 hours a day. Called humanly! Now, many people think that what I did was not human either! And I was worth sitting in the cell 23 hours a day. Yes, certainly, many people are reading these lines. But now that I've been in freedom for almost ten years, I'll look a bit different on that matter. If authorities are detaining a person! Failing all responsibility on these authorities to ensure that it is taken both physically and mentally well.

Chapter 22

Many times, one hears that a detained attempted to kill himself or even of successful. Why do you just happen to get revenge, do you believe? You can also see it from the side of the suspect who likes the bus locked as they usually feel threatened. But it's there! As the whole system falls, I think!

Because a prosecutor arrests the perpetrator, the victim is invaded by false security. The suspect may feel safe for a while during the arrest itself. But when the trial will start, if there is a trial at all! Is there a major reason why the victim may feel a more significant threat picture, for what happens when a police report is received, the police who receive the notification usually promise gold and green meadows to the victim, but reality taps quickly and appears in a completely different form.

The truth is that the suspect is locked on completely inhumane conditions, and it creates a person who becomes extremely revengeful! Because the suspect can not meet someone and become isolated, people begin to think completely crazy thoughts. Which makes you suspectly short-thought. You do not have to keep a person locked for a longer period of time, because people like to start breaking down! And there that man becomes like a ticking bomb.

The fact that in our modern society treats suspects in this sick way is strange. Then this country is a great advocate for those human rights. If you are arrested, you should be considered innocent until the sentence falls. How many people do you think do not be herded every year in Sweden which is then released when it is found that they are not owed, these lines do not contain the crimes I have made or why I have been arrested. If you are rude, you can count on these coercive measures. With these lines, I want to enlighten ordinary people that they can easily be herded. It is common practice that high officials have been arrested due to suspicion of eco-crime. These high officials live a life in the so-called reckless corridor. Which means! The fact that such a person is detained can have only devastating consequences, since a detention gives extremely bad reputation for these people. But probably the worst! Is such a person's psyche unable to cope with this deprivation of liberty, they feel very bad of this and go into some kind of psychosis and lead to suicide attempts. Even a routine buse is crazy, no matter how tough they are! The difference is just that buses usually have a detention in the game rules, as they perform different crimes. Thus, the bus's psyche is more prepared. And it is usually absolutely crucial.

Now I do not want the authorities to be deprived of these coercive measures. I think they should train staff who have special skills in this area. The prosecution service often goes out in mass media, with their staff being specially trained in this area. But how can they be specially trained as they have not themselves been exposed to this form of detention? Should the prosecution be able to develop, the staff must know what it's like to be locked up without knowing when they even come out. Why not have it as part of their education. Let them sit for 2 weeks or a month. Let them feel their own feelings, which are clearly evident in isolation. Then they would not have been so unpleasant to those who were hiding anymore. Because there are a large percentage of people arrested and who are innocent and, they are treated equally as the heavily criminal persons.

The differences are great between a villain`s psyche and a Smith. A villain has it as a job, while a Smith, who is accidentally arrested, loses the footsteps in total. But back to the event ...

I was sitting in the prison cell and wondered how long I would have to sit there. I knew that the prosecutor could not hold me longer than the period of imprisonment would be. But with that backpack I pulled on! So, any kind of shatter could be a long time behind the bars.

For that it is! A normal person would have a couple of months for unlawful weapons possession, for example. Should I personally be punished for a similar crime! Should it be at least 6 months! No matter what the law says. That sounds unreal but that's the truth. Certain criminal elements become harder punished than others. But now I began to plan how to survive this arrest period, purely psychic! And without losing the mask against the guard. I was hard as granite when I was in contact with them. Instead, I was soft, like a little bumblebee, and felt very bad! Anyone who has locked on this insulation form has tears in abundance. But no one would like to admit it. Hardly I want to admit it myself. I only start after a week, in this cell fall into my own psychic swamp and where you hit the bottom with noise and bang. You never get used to being locked up, and whether you've been locked X times! Then break down a bit for each time. You get stronger than a normal person, but never so strong so you do not know it. Should you become indifferent, it's time to visit a particular department at the hospital, as you obviously are not fresh anymore.

The days went extremely slowly and, I wanted to talk to someone as person and person as I did not get crazy. Sitting for 23 hours locked up makes a temporary mess and can not be explained, but you have to experience this hell yourself. One day one of the guard comes and opens the door to my cell and wondering how I was doing? This was in the evening and then there are regulations that say the guard should be two when they open the cell door so late! Due to the fact that the personal worship is minimal. Especially when they opened the door to a person who was subjected to complete restrictions. We could imagine being extra desperate to accommodate. Then he made a misconduct, but it showed! That there are also good guards. He put a chair in the middle of the entrance to the cell door. He had noticed that I started to floor after more than two weeks locked and completely insulated. He said you could get a prison priest who could come and talk to someone if you wanted to. Should I speak with a priest about the church and the like?

No! This obviously seemed ridiculous. I could not sit and talk to a priest. You knew what he was talking about. Then he would like to become a Christian too! Then this guard says that this priest is not a regular one. He never mentions the church or his faith. Unless you say it yourself. Really? I wondered at the plight. How is he then?

He's just here to help them get in when it's heavy and if you want someone to talk to. The guard said he thought I could try to talk to him. Then he said that the priest had a confidentiality, which he thought would fit me perfectly. This guard had had many heavy criminals who lived on organized crime. After a long conversation with that guard, we decided that I would try to talk with him. The day after in the afternoon, I hear how they open my cell door. There was the guard that I talked to the night before, and he brought a little red-haired priest. But I could not look at his clothes! Since he had no evidence that he was a priest!

But I did not have any other visits that were instantly booked. Now I was like a proud teet up! Ice cold and with a glance that probably said I could handle myself. Fixed the truth was a completely different one. However, I was somewhat fond of this priest, when it was impossible to see if he was what he declared to be! He could be a clue that took advantage of the situation when I was down for countdown. I was very suspicious of this person. I did not know if I could trust him. He was clearly used to the priest being met with great suspicion. When the priest entered the cell, he introduced himself, then he said no more. The plump went and there I sat with a priest who did not say a sound. The whole situation began to be embarrassing and I did not want to say anything, then you would be cool. 5 minutes walk, then the priest said he would not talk about religion and, asking why that was why I was quiet. No! I answered as cold as an icebreaker! He asked if there was anything I wanted? How do you mean? Did I ask the priest?

Then he wondered if I had any interests. I answer that I played the piano since a lot of years and thought it gave me a lot. So good, the priest! Then I may arrange so you can get a synth in the cell! Yes? I responded very well! Given that I was subjected to restrictions and it would in principle be asked if you would like to change your bags or go to bed. Either so did he drive with me? Or I was wrong! Then I was pretty cooked in my head after 2 weeks of isolation. But then the priest told me that he could return during the morning with a message. Which he actually did!

He was so routine to carry heavy criminals! He knew that he had to build up a trust. Because he really came with a synthesizer the following day! I thought he seemed to be one, of the kind you could trust. But I was very suspicious of him. But clear that he would have a chance! Though I was very uncertain. It could be a form of psychological play as the prosecutor lay behind in some way. That I did not think clearly, you can really take it first now! When it sounds like I was almost manic and suffered from persecution.

The prison priest left the synthesizer and hoped that I would benefit greatly from it during the detention! But also said he came back in a few days. He called the bell so the guard would open the door, so he could go. When the guards come, he asks if I want to go for a while in the exercise area. It felt like a good suggestion. A suggestion I thanked for! The guard says he will be back soon and that he will secure the corridor. Securing the corridor meant that the guards would close my inspection hatch and then ensure no other interns were or could get out of the corridor while I was there. I can understand if it's hard to imagine how it felt to me emotionally! Then I've been insulated for so long. But getting into a corridor without people is strange, when my whole body screamed to see someone. Before the guard opened to me, I could hear the cell, how the guard communicated with his colleagues. It could sound like this!

Central guard! I have a red internal, is it clear that I can open the door? One minute! A green is coming from the exercise area. The guard awaits his colleague! Then you heard that Red intern could come out! When the guard then opened the door, it was to touch the legs!

Then we had a good way down the corridor and then into a form of locking door, then up for a staircase. When you got up the stairs there stood an extremely high stack of slippers!

As you would wear when you went out to the exercise area. Outside the exercise area, there were green tarpaulins that were for us who had restrictions and who did not see any other people than the guards.

Tarpaulins that were taken after the Red intern went out into the exercise area. You were treated as an animal. Even the difference between animals and red interns was that animals did not have green slippers.

It is quite sick that you have to deal with people in such a way in this country. That you can legally break down people so is absolutely incredible. But in the guidelines for the detention they are called to protect any innocent people from being seen in the prisons. Certainly, it sounds good when you see it from a more political perspective. The reality is another.

I was usually kindly treated by the guards, when they knew we never bothered when we were locked up. The game was like over! So there was no reason to give up on them. Then they just did their job just like everyone else. But sometimes it happened that it ran over, so I did not feel comfortable sitting there locked.

I remember especially once, when it was time for supper and the caravan rolled in the corridor. I just knew where in the corridor the caravan was located. Though you put in his cell. It was heard of the joints in the floor that the carts rolled over. Earlier in the day I prayed to let the inspection door open! Then it became very enclosed and dry air in the cell. The ventilation was no elevation. You got very dry lips. It was so bad air that the plagues shared the defense's lipstick. But now it was dinner and it also meant that the night shift went on for the night.

146

Chapter 23

When the trolley arrives at the cell before mine, the guard closes the inspection door again. It was the drop that caused the cup to flow over. My aggressiveness was high and I threw it plastic chair that stood inside the cell against the wall. This rage outbreak was more than heard in the corridor. Then the guard opens the door and says I'll shut up. That was his biggest mistake that day. I feed several fist strokes against the plague who had my face in the middle of the inspection hatch. The piece was strangely insane when he realized that I was really angry. They would not even open the cell door. Then they sent another guard! To stand with the face in the inspection hatch! And that would calm me down! It took time I can say before I went down the lap! I was so angry, so I was daring. Though it was just a sketch. But it just proves that people should not be so isolated, when you get easier to say the least. I had met the edge of the inspection door myself and pushed the knot on my little finger through repeated strokes. The fingers and the rest of the hand had already begun to swell again. The guard that came back a little later with a tray of food would look at my hand when he saw that it was not right. Normally, I would not get this personal food service, so the guards come in with a tray. This made this guard because of the occurrence, and that they did not consider it appropriate to open my cell door when I had my rage outbreak. Probably it was a wise decision! When you do not know how it ended. The guard said quite promptly that he thought the nurse would check her finger and her hand the next morning. He wanted to give me a painkiller so I could sleep during the night.

But I did not want that. In the morning the nurse came.
She barely entered my cell from she said that a doctor
should look at it. She looked and pushed a little gently on
my little finger who was painful, but when the nurse asks
about it hurts a lot? Had I had to answer that barely felt at
all! Probably something she did not believe in. The doctor
came in the afternoon to examine his hand. He
immediately said that the hand would radiate at the
hospital immediately. Now it may sound easy, but it is
never popular with the planners to take a detention, in the
civilian, as space risk is significant.

But it had to wait another day when it was late in the
afternoon. The guards would change shifts and it was not
a life-threatening harm. So, I had to go there for two days
before I could get to a hospital for examination. It was not
good! The doctor was not happy about this displacement
when he did not know if I had something broken in my
hand. It was after all the one who was responsible for his
patient, if there were any permanent damage due to the
time shift. But just wait for the next morning. Early the
next morning, a guard came in order to say good morning
and to watch so I was okay! With the exception of the
hand. I was informed that I was going to the hospital after
breakfast and that I would get a new washout before we
left. So, it was to throw breakfast in a hurry, then change.
Now came the guard to open my cell door. When he
opened the door, I saw that there were two guards. Now
their empathy came forth when they would have to put on
my handcuffs. They thought it felt wrong, considering
that my right hand was very swollen. But they just could
not take me without handcuffs, that's how easy it was.
They did their best because it would not push that much.
When wearing handcuffs! Should the one who puts on
them, be sure to lock the boots so they can not pull to

gether! More than they are at your own setting. They do it by pressing a small stick, similar to a sprint, but it is mounted in the handcuffs itself. This is a security, not the handcuffs should be able to stop the blood flow itself, as a handcuff can be compressed in any way.

We start to go down the corridor and then take the elevator down to the police's garage, they share a garage with the police. Then I had to jump into the prison Volvo's combi as they used for this kind of transport. It only took 10 minutes until we arrived at the hospital. Now it should be parked as close to the entrance as possible. This of safety concern. If I'd get for myself to try to escape from these guards. I did not have a mind to accommodate when I had to be out in the community, if only for a short period of time, I enjoyed it. Well inside the hospital! Went one guard up to pay the patient fee. There were clear routines on such hospital visits when the police informed the nurse in the gap that they were from the Criminal Care. Which would give us a fortune, it was supposed! The other guard was kind enough to set me out to the side so, it would not seem so much. He even pulled his arms on the shirt over the handcuffs so, it would look less waking up.

Standing staring at a board hanging on a wall, you can do it a while. But after a quarter it starts to feel extremely stupid, no matter how good the guards mind was from the beginning. I was just waiting for us to go to the X-ray department, so I would come from this ugly and abstract art that hung on the wall. Now we should start to go X-rays to sit outside and wait for it to be my turn. The guards sat on one side of the corridor. They took a newspaper that would help them to slow down the time. It turned out that they both were very hunting interested. They did not detect the slightest form of excitement or stress. Which I thought felt good, since you can often get beginners to show how successful they are to keep track of the bus. These guards were so calm as a human could be. As we sat there waiting for an old man, walker further down the hall. He did enough for 3 km an hour and then it was fast. As he began to approach the benches outside the x-ray where we sat and waited, the old man looks at me! I greeted what he did. Then, when he saw my handcuffs, it was like that walker was suddenly driven on nitrous oxide. For the old man increased from 3 km to at least 85 km. Probably, he was a little worried when he saw the handcuffs. Or the disc brakes had completely loosened on the roller. Well, because it looked a little fun! The one guard said to the old man that he could calm down and there was no danger! But the man proceeded rapidly. Now it was my turn to get into X-rays. One of the guards goes straight through the entire X-ray, then sitting in the same room as the staff, while the picture was taken. The other would stand outside the entrance door to the X-ray. But now the first problem came! The left handcuff does not want to open the guard did its utmost to make it go. The guard then asked the nurse if I could not hold it on my hand when it was my right hand that would be X-rays? Absolutely not said the nurse decided. This guard was then called on his colleague to see if they could solve the problem together! They could not just go anyway. It took at least 5 minutes to get off the handcuff. By the time, a nurse could come up to put my hand right so, they could take the pictures. The nurse looked there for a little excited. She was very nice, but in a more excited and nervous way. No wonder! A nurse alone with a raw bus! Clearly, she was a little worried! Though she had no pain to expect from me. Now it was time to go out and sit down on the bench to wait. It took several hours before we got any message. Nothing was broken but the finger should be pulled by a doctor. So, we had to go to emergency, where we patiently had to wait again.

When the doctor comes in, he says after checking the X-ray plates! That he would try to pull right my finger that had been offset by the repeated strokes. The doctor said that you can stumble, but it does not matter if an anesthetic feels quite good in one finger. I decided not to take the stunning spray.
The doctor sits on a chair in front of me and grabs for a moment around my right arm and then for a while around my finger. Now it will feel the doctor said! That's okay I said! As in any pathetic way, it would be extraordinary for the moment. The doctor pulled his finger with a knot! I can say so much! Those words that came out of my mouth were not taken directly from a psalm. It hurriedly hurt. If I had any color on my face, it was still pale. The doctor asks how it felt when I touched my finger? I answer that felt okay! Though I was a bit taken from the pain that occurred when the doctor pulled the right finger.

Chapter 24

We should now go back to the detention, again to be locked in my cell.

I had begun my third week at this isolation time and you only fell down for every day that went into the psyche. It was as one's brain ceased to be active and did not even hurry to get the impression that one could get as confronted with complete restrictions. It was not even fun to play music. Nothing was interesting anymore. The guards started to understand that I was suffering from sleep deprivation and calling a doctor who was willing to give me something to sleep on. The doctor wrote a tablet that would help. But when the guard came to give me that tablet, I did not want it. He then summoned an old and experienced guard who had a lot of experience with the lack of sleep and the problems that could arise. This guard was good! He did not start by saying that I would take the tablet, but instead tell me what could happen if I did not sleep for a long time. It was not nice at all! When he tells how the brain step by step shut off and finally only went to the reserves. This guard could break a psychologist in a quarter. He was really good at his job. He was so good so, he made me take the tablet. When I took the tablet, the guard said he thought it was nice to talk with the bus from Skåne, when he had most heard and seen the kind of bus via the media. We talked well almost an hour after taking the tablet. But now Persson began to get tired! Really heavily tired! I had to tell the guard to get out of my cell when I had to sleep.

I fell asleep and slept five quarters an hour. I missed the breakfast and then you really should be tired if a Skåning(countryboy) is going to miss a meal!

The guards did not want to wake me because they knew I

had slept badly for some time. It was almost so I began to think that these guards had a human riot. I did not want to take tablets because I did not like being affected by a lot of chemicals. But that tablet was a healthy investment for my own health. I felt much better the day after. It is completely unassuming how sleep failure can affect a person. One does not think about the meaning of sleep, so you can understand the importance of good sleep. But without it, you're just a boiled vegetable. It was even so good that I hurried to sit and play some music on the syntercizer that the priest had taken there. Time was heavy! The clock did not move directly. I knew what the whole thing was about, with the arrest itself. That the Prosecutor would receive recognition from me in a trial. But he could look in the blue. Had he driven me so far into the mental swamp, he would not get any recognition of me anyway. I had to work with something, so I had time to go. One could work with the manufacture of clothing clips inside the cell. It was to put together small clothes nails for clothes hangers that would keep the children's clothes on the hanger. That work consisted of laying a plastic piece, then a steel spring. Then you had to tension that spring with a similar screwdriver. Then put a new piece of space and finally release the feather. And then you would have made a clothes tip! For each pair of clothes, I put together, I received 3 pence for. There were no bigger sums, but I did it because I would have time to go. But even because you would not break up overall. There were also other jobs, such as making holes in road signs with a large cavity where you had to have a long iron pipe when you were to push the hole collector. I asked if I could do it instead. But the Central Guard and the guards did not dare give me a long iron pipe. They considered me to be in favor of this work.

Too bad I thought, as it was much better paid per sign. But I understand their decisions now afterwards more than well.

I began to realize after 3 weeks of isolation that I would stay for a while. And I began to imagine that you had a long time to expect behind lock. I was now inside my fourth week and my brain had begun to get used to this life. I had now got a tv on my cell. Now the prosecutor seemed more human. He even made sure to move to the suite. The suite is a cell with its own toilet and shower and is used primarily for captivated women with small children. But now you got a bit better. One had the clean luxury with tv toilet and shower. Now it was party! You could play Bingolotto and see Wanted. For a normal person, it certainly does not sound so luxurious, but believe that this is luxury in the unlocked world in double sense. That's how I even thought the bed was more beautiful, though it's exactly the same model. It was a good idea to take a shower and watch TV. Which I did. Everything was much better than before. One night when you sit there watching TV. I hear a bad bang of something falling apart, inside the cell side of mine. You did not think so much about it at first. But then I thought it was heard as someone was amazed Help help me! At first, I thought that you began to be careful due to the isolation. But when I screwed down the sound on Tv. Could I by placing my ear towards my cell wall toward the neighbor's cell, hearing a man who seemed to have severe pain. The first thought was that he tried to hang him self. But in a detention cell there is not much to hang in. Because they are designed so, just because it will not be possible to suicide. But though you knew that, you were not sure. I waited a few minutes to hear if he continued shouting or

154

if the person was calm down. I could not tell why the person did not call the Central Guard if he was hurt or had a bad time. After about ten minutes, I decided to call the central guard. Then this person had screamed in intervals and it did not seem like he could call the guard himself.

When the Central Guard responded, they clearly wondered what I wanted, as I did not usually hear from me immediately. I explained that the person to the right of me obviously has big problems and screaming for help all the time more or less. The central guard asks if I slept badly again? No! He has a problem, but now I have told you! Okay said the guard! I send down someone to check it! After a minute, I hear a guard coming, with its two-wheel drive you can kick off one foot! I heard that the guard did not drive past my cell. Damn I thought! Now it was wrong. My right side was my left when you were in the corridor. I just heard that the guard opened the cell door on his right side. There was not the guard especially welcome. He closes that cell to open my inspection hatch to hear why I called and said someone needed help? I told the guard that it is the next cell. We felt just as stupid! Then this misunderstanding arose. He closes my inspection door to open the other cell door. The guard finds a man lying in bed just screaming with pain. It turned out he had a serious back injury and could not get out of bed to call the guard. He was so glad that the guard came. The guard said it was his neighbor who informed the central guard and asked them to come to his cell. Now there was a good move in the hallway and the ambulance staff came to pick up the guy. The doctor considered it necessary to bring the person to the hospital. But already the next day, the guy was back and left a big thank you to me, via the guard! Because I had called so he got help.

Strange to help a person you had not seen even, but just heard. But it was nice that he appreciated my little one bet.

It was December month and Christmas, was in anticipation. A feast where you usually think a lot about your family and not least on their children. I felt very bad that I could not be with my children, then I want to give them a Christmas present and celebrate Christmas with them. Such a festive day was hated no less against the notifiers. I had tried to do my best by sending letters often to my children and especially before Christmas.
Remember all the letters I received from my children during all detention.
But I especially remember a letter from my little son Alexander!

Chapter 25

Alexander started the letter!

Hi dad!
Have a question that makes me angry! Who's the stupid person who opens my letters I get from you Daddy? I want to say to the stupid person that you can not open my letters, call the police otherwise ... is the ball heavy to go with the bone dad the ball and the chain around your leg dad?

I was almost completely destroyed by this letter, which my little son wrote to me. The tears sprayed straight out, there were tears, so you could almost believe that you had a built-in high-fat wash in your eyes. But also, a heavy, angry, depressing feeling, which suits me all the way. It hurt so badly and severely in the soul. A feeling that almost made a paralysis. I loved my children so much and why had I now exposed them to this misery? I could not even defend myself mentally anymore by thinking about what, like made me this evil and devilish person. Why did not I stop this development? I could not even think the tears ran uninterruptedly. I just wanted to die! In order to get rid of these painful feelings that I now completely bathed in.
I had to delete the letter! What my son meant that the letters were opening was that the prosecutor read all my outgoing mail. So, I could not complicate the investigation. Then they just taped the letter and sent it to my children. But that was exactly what my son did not like.

Afterwards, I have seen those letters I sent to my children during this time. And it was a little odd how I had written many letters, differently, but with the same content. I know that on several occasions I really wonder before I wrote, so I had new things to tell me about. But it was like the brain just twisting the same things all the time, but with different sentences. Very strange indeed.

There you sat on Christmas Eve! What could I do about it? Nothing could be done! The guards came with Christmas dinner, a little later in the afternoon. It was a Christmas table that few Swedes can afford to get on. Four full wagons full of food! I have never seen so much Christmas food at once. I can guarantee that there was no Christmas dish that was not on these carts. When the guard opened my cell door, and I got to my surprise to see these carts I was really excited.
And Skåning as you are! Then you love Mad! (Food) I took two big plates and a little full of food, then I only had to take it once. It would be stupid not to take away all this good food.
I could easily say that the meal itself was the highlight of this Christmas Eve night. The lack of children was untidy, A feeling I would not even expose my worst enemy to. No one is worth feeling such a feeling. That I put myself in this situation myself is sure many think. What I can understand! But whatever turns the hedge, it sits behind, and you feel most sorry for yourself.
But like all Christmas, it ends and the middayers come. But it felt like it was Christmas, Midweek or any other holiday. It was as bad in the cell for it. I had a psyche that was almost neutral to everything and everyone. I would just survive myself.

After five weeks of isolation, it was now time for the trial. I started to pick myself up again when I felt coming outside these walls. Though I was going to trial, it was what felt good. Perhaps because I saw that there would be some kind of judgment and decision about my immediate future. The prisoner's staff came three of them, to pick me up. Yes, they did not trust me. It showed them clearly with the number of accompanying plots to the trial. So, it was just the handcuffs and go to court. The claiments did not seem to. They sat in an adjoining room and did not go out of court to start. I had apparently put such horror in these people so, they would not confront me more than was necessary. The right asked if I was the accused person, as certified by my Attorney. Then the prosecutor began to explain what crimes he thought I had done. The right then asks me how I respond to these statements as the prosecutor recently reported? My lawyer replied that his client denied crimes on all points. The court appeals to the Prosecutor to ask him to prove this by means of technical evidence, as well as the plaintiff's own statements. The prosecutor then brings out my baseball tree, as part of the technical evidence, saying that the suspect has threatened people with this baseball tree and to break the knee bowls on the claiments. Which Prosecutor forces with one of the claiments own stories. My Attorney says there are no witnesses or other evidence that strengthens the claiments story! The prosecutor then puts in a comment that this claiments had already described the suspected baseball tree in detail during the first notification. The right then asks me how I intended to explain the claiments detailed description of my baseball bat? I answered the right! That he could have seen the baseball tree as he passed my car, which apparently stood below his apartment. Then I said!

You can not lock people in possession of a baseball tree. Then the state will lock in every Baseball team in this country.These comments, in essence, created a great deal of irritation at the Court.

The court now asks the prosecutor if he had a more substantive reason for this prosecution. The prosecutor then replied that he recently received this case from another prosecutor. Therefore, no further evidence had emerged during the preliminary investigation. Now the right was badly annoyed at the Prosecutor who was so vague grounds and above all, had the suspect arrested for a long time. The court reasoned a little and found out to dismiss the entire prosecution, since there was no one as a complete technical evidence. But also, that the right by seeing it on Objective Reasons could not help me and put down the prosecution on all points. The right informs me that I am entitled to compensation for the time I have been detained. I said I did not want any compensation. Which probably surprised a lot! But you should not overlook too much, I thought! Now the court was empty in a few minutes. I had to go back to the prison to pick up my clothes and other belongings that I had to leave at the time of detention. When we got back to the prison, I got a nice look at the cell and I was even taking a shower before leaving the detention. But when I got into the cell again, the guard said that they had to lock me in when the rules were so. But it was probably the only time I could say that it was okay that they locked. Then I knew I would soon be out of this hell. At last you were in freedom again! That I was free now felt absolutely wonderful! And then you might think that I had enough of this criminal swamp? But not!

I took the train home from that city, because I did not want my car at the moment, because I thought it was too hard to sit in it. I was determined to just go home to my apartment. When I got home, I threw my on the couch and began thinking about how I could do smarter things and that gave them the really big dollars. That I had now got a name was not the least hesitation. But what reputation and name you had then! Would get any Svensson to become dark red. But at this time, I had no problem with rumors, it was even a brand at that time and a prerequisite for survival. I had a lot of thought on Ekobrott as the right planned could give a huge return, as it's called. But I was, of course, limited, knowledgeable, in business administration. A knowledge that could hardly give better success to major corporate corridors. I decided to scramble important things like financial reports, month, quarter, tertiary, 6 months and beyond.

I was completely obsessed with this financial knowledge, and that really interested me deeply. I had no books on this particular subject so I ordered books but also read a lot via the Internet, as this could give a broader picture of how this financial world worked well.
Everything that started with the word Tax Planning I read several times, thus finding all possible loopholes in the law. I was now in part of the crime where I would make it illegal, completely legal and with existing laws performing the crimes without the authorities being able to intervene with any coercive measures. As I said earlier, there is no perfect crime. And it will never do either. Certainly many who have been exposed to me will certainly claim the perfect crime.

But the question is? How do you define the perfect crime? Many would surely describe it by saying that, for example, you had made a burglary, sold the things, retained the money from the burglary without entering. Certainly! Quite economically, one could say that it was a perfect crime, but I do not share such a reasoning. Then I consider! If something is perfect, it should not hurt anyone. Neither economically, mentally or physically. Such a crime does not exist! Making a crime with financial gain is no problem, and without the law catching you. An authority that knows this possibility is the Public Prosecutor. But also the police authority. Both of these authorities get frustrated and look at when the crimes happen more or less without being able to intervene. Due to the fact that the buses know and can make the book. By utilizing these skills, an intermediary is created, with society on one side and the buses on Other. Because the buses do not cross the line proving that a crime has been done, but instead balances the line of law and where this line represents the difference between crimes or legal. Then there will be an alleged crime in a whole new day. The prosecutor shall again prove that a crime has been committed. But how should this prosecutor do it? No, just that! The prosecutor can not prove that. Many who read these lines may think this is a nonchalant description how easy it is to deceive our legal community. But that's not about it! I now want more that society will introduce greater flexibility in its law enforcement. There will always be a bus to catch another bus. If you look at the statistics of the state on various crimes and really examine them carefully, most common people will get a shock. Because of the crimes that are cleared up, the smaller crimes are cleared up. The fact that the state does not cope with organized crime is a fact. But when they read their statistics, they show that the law works and that most buses go behind lock and bomb. Why not know the facts instead! The state, in consultation with BRÅ (Crime Prevention Council), should be able to arrive at a more sophisticated solution, in which they instead took on the experiences and skills of old buses. It is guaranteed the only safe solution that can yield tremendously good results. It may require some adjustments in the law or the like. But if society wants to catch those really big crooks, society must begin to work with

ex-crooks instead of putting sticks in the wheel! Old crooks are not let into society because of their backpack. This is not due to lack of skills! On the contrary, I would like to say. In order for an old crooks to get into a company, the risk is extremely high that this crooks skills are completely overcome ordinary employee. Thus, we have another problem. No crooks will take my job, sure many ordinary people will say. But now it's not the question of getting each other's work apart. No! it is for the state to appoint new strategies and modern measures against organized crime.

Chapter 26

During my most criminal time, I often wondered how the state thought when trying to reduce heavily organized crime. Fighting a crime that exploits the flexibility to one hundred percent with a square and outdated system. It's just as stupid! Like driving into a gasoline tank and fueling diesel in a gasoline engine. It does not work! The prosecutor's office is screaming for more prosecutors and the prime minister adds more money to an already inoperative system. At the same time as the Public Prosecutor's Office is expanding its cooperation at a more international level.

Is the legal community not aware that they actually, with these measures just throwing money into the lake? What is so hard to understand? Because the Prosecutors get more muscle economically! Can they only investigate more, but also just establish that crime is, increasing and by expanding the prosecutors' powers at the international level, we only get an effect that would correspond if you put the team's arm on a bench. Where this arm reaches much longer, but with a muscular function that is long and not functional.

The most extreme could be, for example, if the Minister of Justice could think of getting up from his chair and going to his place office window, bend on the neck and look down on the ground. For those on the ground they go to the ex-crooks who have the solution to law enforcement. Is convinced that many crimes could be resolved, for example, Criminals got a chance to show what they are going for, in a legal way. Through such

cooperation, we soon had a society with less crime and
effective law

enforcement. Not to the State and the former crooks
cooperate largely due to fear and poor communication.
But even the law looks like it does. However, because the
decision-makers are in the guarded nest, communication
can not occur when the solution is on the street and the
decision-makers are in the corridor of society. It would be
significantly better if politicians with decision-making
rights were able to find a form of neutral platform, under
the leadership of government, to assemble a team based
on routine police officers and ex-crooks who know how
to walk around the team. Did any politician dare to do
this! Had we had an extremely efficient work done and
the community could have regained many beautiful
taxpayers, which now end up on foreign bank accounts
where the team's arm is purely borderless, but nothing can
do.
The state seems to solve social problems in one way, and
law enforcement on another. How often do not you hear
when journalists ask questions to different politicians that
they will appoint an investigation or purely by a
commission to address the problem. But the thing is a
little strange when politicians always, in the event of
social problems, add their so-called Experts. But they do
not do that in law enforcement, they use professional
trained police officers and professors to do the job. When
the real pros are, they crooks who chose to be honest. No!
Basically, this country is going to be knocked if we got an
effective system of large and organized crime.
Should the state dare to attack those big crooks, high
officials had been found sitting on their high chairs in our
business. These people with a lot of power in society
would not be able to handle their illegal business while at
the same time sitting in the threads that take care of

Swedish security policy and who direct the common human rights community in the direct descending direction. I've seen too much of this corrupt society to keep my mouth shut longer.

Many times people say that they must tell you that someone gets it. If an event where something terrible has occurred. The problem is only! To just ANYONE, are those who are most corrupt in society. With much power and great influence. Who will you tell? If just such an event?

If we play a little with the thought, and that the state would get more effective law enforcement. This would lead to extremely high unemployment in, for example, the Criminal Services.

Because it's built today, it can be compared to a garbage dump that takes care of everything that can be recycled. Exactly, the prosecution works today. You are sentenced to a sentence and then released without income or accommodation. Which leads to society being filled with recidivisms of recidivism, as they can not afford themselves in any other way. This recycling system is funded by taxpayers and reimbursement tax. Meanwhile, as the usual "Smith" naively believes that "Uncle The, State" takes care of the country's legal community, they run the confidence chosen and save their money in The, "tax haven" and this is called a democratic justice society! No! I'll Quote a great Swedish artist PEPS PERSSON with the song False Math! Because that's exactly what it is! Yes! Comments are really superfluous! But someone must open mouth, and actually enlighten how reality looks. Maybe pity it must come from a ex. criminal. Or, it's necessary for people to wake up and realize the facts. But back to the story ...

Chapter 27

I began to understand the importance of all these financial reports that would be an important part of a possible eco-robbery. But being able to read a big business's interim reports can be described as much like reading an electricity bill. It's possible to do, but I'm not easy to say. But as in real life, you work up, just as it is in the criminal world. One begins with simple crazy crimes and then advances.

When I was most in my financial and criminal world, Mc related people began to appear. Mc related contacts I had previously, but not of this caliber. As through his network of contacts, I had noticed my criminal jobs that gave rise to results. I initially met a big man purely muscularly. In this book he is called Kenna!

This Kenna would be a question if I could meet a member of this organization for closer cooperation. I thought of the ones I used to work for when Oxfilé was done. But this was apparently another clientele with Harley Davidson as the lead star. Now started to get crowded in the kitchen! What or who would I join! The first thought was that the dollar had to control. But that was a naive thought, then this was not an option. Hhm! What should I answer I thought Then I ask this Kenna if you could freelance type like I did before, but he could not answer this. He was only tasked to hear if a meeting was possible and if there was an interest in it. My first spontaneous thought was not to conduct a meeting. But it was enough that I flashed once and saw this big dollar sign when my eyelids were down for a millisecond.

Of course, I wanted to meet this member who belonged to the elite of the world and with a network of contacts that stretched over much of the world. Good, I'll call him now Kenna said! Which surprised me when it would be a meeting right away. Kenna wanted us to go home to his apartment which was about 7 km from my home. When we entered Kennas apartment we took a snack and snacked a bit, pending this member coming. I barely think he lifted the coffee cup before hearing how Kennas's front door opened. I was tense like a feather! I heard someone shouting Tjena! Out of the hall and Kenna answer Wait! Now there was pressure in my brain. It was as though all brain cells in my head had some summit and that occurred between the big and the small brain. Felt like a milder form of oxygen deficiency in the brain. The person who entered the room we call John in this book. This John was now in the room where I and Kenna sat and caught. He only had a regular jacket and not a vest! What is this? I thought!? Then this jacket destroyed my entire picture of this member. There I expected him to have a west. And of course, my jaw could not be closed, but had to ask why he did not have his vest?

John just laughs and says he has his vest under the jacket. As he now takes off to show where he came from. It felt like someone drove a vacuum pump into my lungs and sucked all air. I did not get a sound. Just a meter from me stands a full member. The feeling I felt might be described as when an art dealer finds a famous artist's undamaged artwork and is now standing in front of this object. The reason he did not have the West visible was because he did not want to draw attention, but also that he came by car instead of his bike. There was a rule that said they should only have their vests on if they drove high. Should they be beaten by another member driving by car and west on or went to town with the west. The guilty club fund was 5000 kr in fines. This was a way for the club to make the members less visible as nobody would pay these fines. John says they followed my latest job! And they were very impressed by how smart these crimes were accomplished. And this without getting stuck! I had a brand that I now found out. Everyone who talked about! That they heard about my crimes! Said that I, as a person, had the ability to turn to, disappear and never again be seen.

Yes! Then maybe I'll answer John! You're impressive, John said! And the club wants to invite you to discuss a little business and where you can earn heavy money on simple things. I would like to respond to that invitation before John had completed the question. Then it became a lot of shit about everything and nothing. Before joining John, he said he looked forward to seeing me in the club in a couple of days. You can trust that, I answered him. John goes to drive away with the car he brought. Kenna already started to point out that I would not go out to the clubhouse if I was not sure I would handle the pressure, as there was no return. Once in, never out!

Though I knew I could not back if I came to their clubhouse, I did not hesitate for a second. Although it was known that a departure would be associated with a safe burial. I had picked up the so-called elite. Something one sought for throughout his criminal time. Once you had gotten a foot in this organization, you would certainly show your feet on all levels. It turned out that they would test one at all levels. What skills you had. I was, computerized so I thought this would be difficult. The only thing beyond my computer world was the martial arts that I practiced for many years.

But that martial arts would soon appear to be slightly thin. In particular, they wanted to see how strong my loyalty was.

I was now at the gate of the clubhouse, which was locked with a thick iron chain and a padlock. But in front of the gate lay a similar thick electric cable. This was no power cable but was a cable that signaled into the clubhouse that someone would pass. Similar to such a cable as the roadworks use when calculating the number of cars passing a certain distance. When I'm standing there waiting for someone to come and open, a policebus slides past my car, on the way further back. They will stop the bus. I thought that Now it's running again. Just when I start thinking about if I was going to lock and boom again, John comes and opens the gate. He waves that I can drive in! When I get out of the car, John comes forward and greets by hand in hand. Then everyone who was in the clubhouse came out to greet the same. One felt really welcome. Everyone was really nice to me. After that, they split their members. John wanted us to go to the clubhouse to see the inside of the club. It was an impressive sight. It was so clean and dust free, so you could lick the floor with your tongue. Everything was neat.
There was everything you could imagine, but what impressed most was the bar with liquor in. It was like looking straight into the liquor store, with all sorts of spirits that were found. An incredible collection. The bar was made in OAK and with a marble slice that was really nice. The bar stools were no IKEA products but were made of stainless steel.
John ask what I liked about their clubhouse. I could only say as it was. Awesome neat! Then I would meet other members who came in afterwards, as I and John spoke.

Everything was military, disciplined and everyone had a role to fulfill. Had Sweden's authorities had half of this discipline we had a whole different society. A society with order and reason!

It was a lot of new impressions that I would take in and I was actually very impressed with how carefully everything was done. I ask John who the President was. John silenced for a second. Then he tells that just who is President, he could not talk when there was a war with another gang. Their President was very much acquainted as this information could cause serious damage to their local organization. To believe you could access who theirs President was, after the first visit, a little naive thought of me. John wanted me to come back as soon as possible. I understood that they had been on my wallet long before I visited this organization. But what their purpose was, I did not know. But it would be a matter of business so much I knew then Kenna's meeting. But what business! I was not aware.

Already the next day, I called John to hear if I was coming to the clubhouse. He thought it was a good suggestion and I started driving quite promptly after we finished the conversation. Out at the clubhouse, John wanted us to talk about what was going on and draw up some sort of agreement on how we were going to work. They do not leave anything by chance there. Which suited me perfectly when I was a person who hated something went wrong or was badly planned. I had a cell phone and a searcher that I would always have with me. Both day and night they would be on. Which built up an inner stress I thought. When you were used to managing your day yourself, and now you were supervised by mobile as well as searchers around the clock. Hm!

Why do you want to belong to such an organization can you wonder? Then it only involves a lot of violence and other illegalities. To me personally, the keyword dollar was what I was crazy about. But also, the big backing that one had behind him. With the knowledge I acquired in my own years, these were now really beneficial. It was the first six months of hell to perform things that I can not list in this book. Then the risk would be directly imminent that the Prosecutor's Office had two Christmases, in the same year and I do not want to give them when I have started a new life. One would pinpoint, train and re-test how much loyalty was against members and the organization was. It was clean brainwashing. But you took it because of what was going to happen. (Thought Man) There was an opportunity to rent a barack at the clubyard. I would like to say a small box, in only 7-8 sqm. It was possible to live in and the cost was 700 kr, which was paid directly to the clubhouse.

One would learn many new rules. Only full members were allowed to attend club meetings, members were not welcome. One would know what was discussed therein. But it was quiet like the wall, about what they had said at the meetings. One was fighting and pulling his straw to the stack during this hard workout, both physically and mentally. It was a matter of being able to cope with the pressure or be totally broken. Since there were a lot of people that would belong to the organization, then the club had to be extra hard in the screening of those who had the potential to cope with this sick workout.
This screening was extreme at our club! And compared to the club that our organization at this time was in war with. Were there big differences. Our rivals had another strategy for weaving new members. It was quite soon to enter the organization if you knew the right people. But

then they also got a mentality on their members that can be described as instability instantly. It was hardly a coincidence that one of their members puts a gun barrel in the head of a small infant at a recovery. Their organization, though, cleans this member himself. But it just proves that it came into anything in that organization with the right contacts. What took five years in our organization took just one year for them. Which creates a crowded person with performance anxiety! Where they at the beginning of their career must show the forefathers by succeeding in their work as DOGS, but also as so-called PACK DONKEYS (Narcotics smugglers) where nobody would fail. Returning to the club as the pack donkey and where you got rid of the package could create devastating consequences for that person. As in such a situation becomes desperate. So desperate that they even put a gun barrel in the head of an infant. Absolutely insane mildly speaking!

Not because our organization was any pious lamb. But to expose children or women to such a thing would NEVER happen. It was an unwritten law that you were under no circumstances exposed to them or even give them an arrow file. One should take care of his family with reverence. At those times there was a problem in a family, the club joined the family. Being under this exercise while having a family, was directly associated with family problems. The club did not accept any abuse or the like in a family. This will be sorted out immediately as soon as the club arrives.

During the probation period, we received weapons training, training on different explosives. Where you would learn what weapons you would use on different occasions or what kind of ammunition was most suitable for a turn. When you learned about explosives, a lot of how to direct the explosion was about to get the effect you're looking for. You were trained in close combat with different weapons such as knives, knuckles with welded small knife blades, and how and where to put these little knife blades into different places on the opponent's body without killing them. Only damage at first stage. There was a member of the organization who had three years in the foreign legion and where he had been the hard soldier training during these three years. We call him Dan in this book.

Then, as a mission, we had to train ourselves in what could be called war art. Where we would learn most about weapons, explosives and fights. It also represents a foreign guy on some occasions during the training itself. Which made me very surprised! But his presence explained quite quickly when this guy, already at the age of 24, was retired on account of mental illness. This mental ill health had occurred during the time he had been in the war between Iran and Iraq. Where this guy had to carry his countrymens dead bodies, and sometimes only parts of them, across the country border so they would come home again. That he was mentally unstable was not much to hesitate about. He had his jerk. Most people had great respect for him, then a life for this guy was absolutely nothing worth it! Seeing the death of the white eye was everyday for him. And as he on some occasions himself said! I'm shooting my own mother for 50 kr no problem! Said he without touching a mine. And I thought that I was feeling distressed. I would be perceived as pure romance compared to this war-injured person.
It was really scary to stand so close to such a person. This person had a strange name, which I do not remember today. But it does not matter! It was in any case that person who would train us in psychological warfare and how to learn how to shut down after doing work. You simply had to learn to erase the unpleasant emotions you

could get at some jobs. Just this part of the education I can now tell you that after all these years it does not work. What they did during this education was learning to confuse things or even shift their feelings. Nothing that I recommend to any living soul. When it comes back, as safe as Amen in the church. Anyway, coming back is anything but fun.

But we will return to the previous topic! Dan began to explain what different hand grenades were available and on what occasions they were used. It was very interesting that education. Then you will get a hand grenade called Distraction Hand grenade, which can be used if you want to shock them. When such a grenade goes off, it becomes an extremely bright light with an extremely high bang. We talk about a noise level of over 150 decibels and a light that completely freezes the outside world for a few seconds. Because this light is so strong, one's entire photocells are activated in the eye and, in turn, creates a frozen image of the outside world. One could compare it to sitting and watching tv and then pressing the pause button. And it's during the frozen seconds that you turn on.
Then we would learn how to optimize the explosion through various proven methods. This he did by showing how a retention worked and through this setting created what was a targeted explosion. It was very crucial for results, depending on how the direction was made. One could learn about many explosives. Pentyl was one of those subjects we learned about. It's a white powder. This agent is used in hand grenades and in many other explosives. It was discussed so much about this Pentyl powder that it eventually became a standing joke among us. When a person could ask if there was Albyl ... No but Pentyl exists! Sick joke, but then it was.

The doctrine of a hand grenade's structure was explained thoroughly. Everything from them different mechanical triggers, chemical stubs to what kind of split grenade consisted of. One had to learn which shells were made of plastic or metal. Which garnets used their casing as splitter and which contained hail, but also those who had their explosive wrapped in a spiral-like spring. One had to learn what explosion the subject had. You counted the volume, energies released by a bang. And it was a blast like C4 where the explosion or how fast the air pressure was moving per second and meter, many say it explode! But few know what an explosion really is. When an explosion occurs, there is a huge mass of energies released. Should a charge of explosive dough C4 explode, it would mean that the air mass and the pressure of the released energies would move at a speed of 8,400 M / s (Meter per second) then you might understand those lines, how powerful Explosion I'm talking about. Many times it is difficult to describe with words how powerful it was. A comparison you can make! If you think is a regular crane truck that lifts up different building materials by running out the actual crane arm. When such a crane arm is pushed out, it is made with a pressure of the corresponding 60-70 kg. Compare it to a shotgun that relieves a regular shotgun. Where the pressure on the hail that comes out is about 600 kg. So then you may understand better.

There was a lot to learn, and I tried to give them a few hours of studying business economics so that they could make them sophisticated eco-robbery beyond.

Chapter 28

Dan finish the day by saying that in the morning we would see one of the world's, most dangerous weapons and could not be revealed. I think like a madman on what weapons it could be. However, there were extremely many dangerous weapons on the market. But a weapon that could not be revealed made it much harder to guess. Then the education began at noon the next day. I was excited about the expectation of this dangerous weapon. Then you get an ordinary daily newspaper? Everyone wondered if it was a joke. Dan is now raising the newspaper to confirm that the newspaper he held in his hand was one of the world's most dangerous weapons. The first thing I thought was about this Dan had smoked bad grass! Very bad grass. And it was not the first of April either. What does he mean I thought, somebody shouts and asks it was what he had learned in the foreign legion to read the newspaper! A comment that made everyone laugh.

Then he began to explain what he meant by this statement after the laugh had passed. He explains that if one rolls one day's paper hard, as hard as it becomes like a thin stick, one could transform an ordinary daily newspaper into a lethal weapon. Which actually works. By tapping the hard-rolled magazine's end point, you can easily kill one person. By striking an oblique nose to the person's nostrils, the person pushes his nose into the brain and the person dies immediately. You could also use this magazine to hurt a person very seriously. This by hitting the newspaper right into a person's eye or in the person's ear. All to harm the enemy. That was exactly what Dan meant with the world's most dangerous weapons.

A weapon no person should reflect on. A magazine that, with simple means, and in just a few seconds became a direct lethal weapon. All this exercise started to affect me negatively purely psychically, since no human is created to act like a machine. I started drinking bigger amounts of alcohol, when this intoxication became a form of relaxation. My body was often the end of all the training and of the psychological brainwash as it actually was. Where in principle you should learn the most about weapons and how to easily harm an enemy on it most efficient way. There were, as I said, many rules to follow within the organization. One rule is that you should not have any form of drug problems. Yes, you read correctly!

Those rules were hard on the club. You had to take drugs, but it would be under controlled conditions, something that anyone could figure out was not working properly. A member! We call him Mirko in this book. Mirko had quite a big problem with cocaine and then he pumped testosterone, which is male hormones. Cocaine and testosterone in combination, everything else is successful. He suffered from a fruitful mood with many aggressive outcomes. Which meant that Mirko was often breaking an additional rule. The rule that said that you could never ever lift a finger against your own brother or otherwise put another brother in danger or trouble. Mirko was close to doing this, many times. Finally, he broke the last, mentioned rule. Inside the clubhouse there was a room called the surveillance room. In that room there were a lot of small monitors (TV sets) where each monitor showed a picture of those surveillance cameras that were mounted on the plank surrounding the clubhouse. Everyone had a certain set time to sit and monitor these cameras. Mirko would go to his pass around three at night and then enter the room where another member sat and supervised the area. When Mirko enters the room, he sees that member sitting asleep. This was among the most serious one could do during the current war period with our rivals. Mirko takes a bottle that he draws to him in his head, then giving him a fat bang. Now the rest of the club woke up, who had to start sharing these two members. Both had now made a very serious crime under the rulebook. What had consequences! Already the same day, they held full members' meeting on this incident, and the rumor quickly emerged that they might be out of the organization. Where the organization put them in BAD STANDING! The worst punishment of all. Which meant that these members would have to leave the organization without any backing and where any other Mc club had to shoot them without consequences. A few days later, it was found that these members received a serious warning and a bet of 10000 kr. A very minor punishment!

Many people thought we had wild parties where we fought and were very deadly. The public had a very wrong picture of organization. Which meant that a decision was made to have open houses where neighbors to the clubhouse could enter. Where the organization offered grilling and spirits. But we had bought a lot of candy and other for any visiting children. The day it was open house wondered many if it would dare come any visitor. Mass media had painted a picture of us, where we appeared as the worst psychopaths. Mirko did not in any way attempt to give us a better picture. When he had seen a minibus a week earlier, a little bit outside of the club gates and where the journalist took a photo of the clubhouse.

When Mirko notices this, he walks and fetches a broom, opens the gate, then walks to the car window on the minibus with the journalist and snaps the wooden shaft into the window. The journalist gets a panic and starts the car, throwing in thc back with full gas. He more or less flies over a little bit and then goes on to the field a few hundred yards before he stops. This panicked journalist wrote no positive lines directly in the newspaper about the organization. Due to this incident, many were doubtful that it would dare to show up any ordinary citizen. There was no immediate rush on the first day. Around eleven o'clock this morning the first visitor appeared. He had one foot inside the gate and the other outside. It looked pretty comic. John began to go against this visitor, the visitor begins to cautiously backwards due to his insecurity and fear he received through mass media. We were crazy and deadly personalities. When John arrived at the visitor, the visitor said he was the closest neighbor to the club yard and started pointing his hand toward his house. John told him that we really liked him to visit. The visitor said then! Yes, that was fun! but now I have to go home. We others were so close that we could hear this visitor's comment about going home. Everyone laughed at when we realized that he was very scared and nervous. We were around six people who now started walking towards the visitor. He was as deserved. But after we greeted him welcome and presented us, he became a little calmer. We are throwing some sausages on the grill, so you can enjoy yourself! Well! Do not know it said the visitor, the lady would have the food ready now, so it may probably be another time. No, come on now! Said John and began to enter the club yard. The visitor looked closely at others with anxious eyes. But later began to go inside. When he had come in about 20 to 30 meters, he suddenly stopped to the contra ry. Here it will be good to grill the visitor suddenly says. It was about a further ten meters to the grill. But we move the grill. The fact that he was staying there was probably because he wanted to see the gate so that he could run out if something would happen.

The visitor was not directly pushing to see the clubhouse. He was still too excited to dare to enter the clubhouse. Everyone really tried to make him relax little and take our invitation correctly. He probably thought we'd kill him. But suddenly it was as his nervousness just disappeared in a strange way. The visitor wanted to enter our local. When he entered, all his injuries were just released. He asked John if he could retrieve his family so they also saw the room. They had a guy who read everything about the organization and was very interested in the headlines and to see how we lived. The visitor said the guy saw everything on tv that was about Mc clubs. Of course, his family welcomed them, as that was the purpose of giving the public a better picture of what we were standing for and that we did not mix ordinary citizens with our business. We wanted to give the public a different picture and explain to those who wanted to hear that we were not as mad as the media meant to us. But convincing these visiting people was not easy. As for several years read about the war we had, it was now for us to be as humble as it could only be.

When the visitor, the closest neighbor of the clubhouse, returned to the rest of his family, felt like the open house the day, was a successful attempt to reach out to those ordinary citizens. The visitor's guy was completely lyrical who finally saw a Mc club in real life and sitting on the bikes. The visitor began to make careful requests if he could cut his grass adjacent to the clubhouse. Something he had not done for a few years due to sheer fear. Everyo ne wondered why he did not cut the grass. Then it turns out that the journalist who recently broke his car had visited this neighbor several years earlier, and built up a fear for us. The journalist had repeatedly pointed out to this neighbor that he would definitely not contact us, and certainly did not show up when this journalist had heard that people had disappeared for smaller things. The whole clubhouse started laugh, when no one had heard anything so funny for a long time. Even this neighbor started laughing now, as he realized that the journalist was just talking crazy. Even his wife laughed loudly, as she also understood that everything was a mass media intimidation tactic. We only had to improve our neighboring relationship. What we did by helping this neighbor with their fence a few days later. The whole thing about having an open house was quite successful! During these days, there were about 15-20 of ordinary citizens, but no entire families directly with children. But in any case, there were some, which most of them were happy with. But after the party, exercise and re-training will come!

We should now be informed of how it looked at the club yard and where somewhere you could talk to the yard without being intercepted by the police. The clubhouse was one of two farms that was most intercepted throughout Skåne. The police aimed at interception equipment against the club yard. What we knew by the Skåne Police Agency leaked information! Like a sieve. There were also rules for this and also for what information could be said in mobile phones. The organization had incorporated equipment for Ericsson phones where you could mount a small encryption device mounted on the bottom of the phone. It looked like a charger fixed wider. By installing this encryption unit, you could then talk to another person without the police being able to hear what we said. This equipment was taken from Israel where war material was easy to get hold of. Since this equipment was directly illegal, and if you use this equipment, which is classified as military material in Sweden, you had to apply for it. Something we obviously had not done.

By training the psychologically, it finally became all this destructive information about how to Handeled weapons, ammunition, interception and psychological warfare became like one's own DNA. You were cleverly fed in the head of all the information and training.
You were drilled so hard that you could take a bullet for your Brothers without even thinking about it. This brainwash became more or less like post-traumatic stress, as soon as we began to think differently than we had learned to think and act. After 6 months in this hell, people had been changed mentally. With a built-in stress, you were always on guard and never knew when to shoot. You were thinking about criminals around the clock and how you could live outside the law. The sense of freedom you sought and where the hoo and dollar played an extremely important role. Had now begun to show in its correct shape. I got stuck in hell!

Like exercise and brainwashing would not be enough! Then too, the police were the pure guns guarding a dead animal on the ground. The police often attacked but rarely succeeded. At the Skåne Police Office, the organization had two police officers who informed us before it would be successful. These policemen are probably managers today. They released information against a sum of money.

Which meant we could get rid of everything before the turnaround. But that's what the prosecutor should do. When the police and their organized crime department hit hard against the clubhouse. They had arranged a wheel loader driving straight through the gates. Then it will sneak over the plank from all corners. Once they were in, they locked everyone in the yard into those garages where the hoars stood when we met them. Then crawl the entire clubhouse for weapons and drugs. But they find nothing then their own colleagues had warned us before. It ended with them getting to the station without anything that the prosecutor could prosecute. But the prosecutor's office was kindly paying the gates by 80,000kr which was completely destroyed when the wheel loader drove through them. Pressure from both the club and police forces makes you hard and empathetic. Living in a world where failure was associated with death or imprisonment creates a machine without feelings. Many who read this probably have difficulty signing in what hell it really was. At the same time being a Daddy was all but easy. One had to try to use the tools they had learned to turn off and turn on. But to be able to shut down, it was required that you had to give up the human vision you once raised to have. A person who is constantly thrown between ingrained loyalty, brotherhood and destruction becomes a bit strange sooner or later. People often felt that they were not in control of their feelings, which consisted of hatred, damage, weapons and the worst of all. The doctrine of rapid liquidation of the enemy if so needed. That we were taught how to get rid of a human body without leaving visible or leading traces included in the training itself. However, that was the only bit that was done on animals. The skeleton of slaughtered animals was used where the bones and skin of these animals had to correspond to a human body. There since they were presented the most effective methods of getting these bones and skin residues to disappear in the fastest and most effective way. Normally, one might think that acid would be the one that would do the job most efficiently. But it's not easiest to get so much acid so it could get a human body to disappear. It was war and in the worst case it might be necessary to have an entire tanker of acid. Something that could not disappear without that the authorities should be alerted. Another problem had been how to store, such an amount of acid.

We became trained not to notice or use visible weapons that anyone would reflect on, as this could be called cops in larger numbers. It was true even now that a useful means could be found that could cause bone and skin retardation to disappear. Finally, it became unleashed lime!

Unleashed lime is extremely corrosive and with some water, as effective as any acid. This lime could easily be bought on the farmers without anyone responding.

As a person, you did not reflect on how sick these tests really were. I was by this team not human but only one machine more or less. I had become even more indifferent to inhuman behavior that any ordinary person had been hardly shocked by. I did worse things than any ordinary person could have nightmares about. Things that were nightmares for ordinary people were my everyday life. My level of tolerance was inhumanly high. A level one can only achieve through years of destructive and empathetic life.

Many of us were struck by unpleasant nightmares. Mirko had the same dream often, a dream where he woke up in a room of rotten human bodies and there had been a panic and could feel the smell of corpse.

I myself had a lot of dreams, but often dreams where you were in the world's freak with different enemies where their goal was to remove one from the earth's surface. I often wake up coldly after fought the worst war with myself. Probably it was the built-in defense instinct which was a must to survive at all.

I remember once i was going to watch when my little boy Alexander was going to play football. After the match, the parents had to go to the boys on the pitch. Behind me comes another dad who recognized me. What he did was he came behind me and put my hand on my shoulder and said my name at the same time. I reigned by direct sweeping away a few meters on the lawn. A pure reflex from my side. Alexander is looking at his Dad and wondering what I'm doing. All parents are watching and removing themselves from the place. I went to the dad and tried to explain that it was a pure reaction. He wondered why I did so? Well, what do you say, It was embarrassing Alexander who was ashamed of his dad, my little guy was angry and thought his dad was stupid, I could not explain to my own son why his own father behaved like the worst gangster, but luckily, children are forgiving their parents after a while, and I am grateful for that. As I said earlier, the free time was something that almost sparked its absence. But of course, you were free, but always accessible.

But on one of those vacant occasions, I was at my apartment when it called the door. I did not check in the peephole of the door but just opened. Outside, the Client stands for Oxfilen and looks really awkward. He wanted to come in! I let him in, and we went into the big room. When we sat down the customer told them they were wondering where I went Then I changed the phone number and did not hear from me since the last shock. I had not had contact with these guys in over six months. The customer began to explain between the lines that one could not just end this clientele. Now I began to realize that we faced a deal in the lower world. I had made my choice and who I belonged to. But the customer was not at all on that line. I told him that I fulfilled my commitment to those with good results. But I also understood that now the results I succeeded now that they would not let me go. I was a good source of income for them. The client said kindly that I would carefully think about my decision. In a friendly way, with a fatal outcome at wrong answers! The customer wondered if I remembered that I asked! For whom did I do the Oxfill shop? Yes, of course, I remember it, I answered him! He explains that it was basically a Russian industrialist who held the threads and he was now angry and disappointed that I just submitted. He wants to meet me soon if I could think of it. I was not at all interested in meeting this man. The customer thought that my response was extremely stupid, since you would not want to get this Russian man. I knew I had backup from the club. But at the same time, you should not expose the club to problems or any single brother for it. It started to be problematic! I knew I could turn to John if I had a problem or if I was wondering when John was taking care of me at this time. When I met John the next time I asked him how to solve this? John said he knew I was working with Russian customers before they became interested in me. John obviously knew more than I knew myself when I did the deal with them. John also says that I must once and for all make up with them, because otherwise you will never get peace and quiet. That John said! Was that I would make up with Russians in the lower world. Well! Hm! Now it was a bit hard! How did John think? Should I go for myself and make up with a Russian businessman and his guard?

Then John says! That I will decide time and place with the Russians as soon as possible. One had the heart in the throat! I still did not know if I would meet themselves or if I had a backup from the club. John would check out the club if they could tell our enemies from the other Mc gang that we were going through their territory. That the clubs would communicate to each other was because it would not be perceived as a war action. An attempt the clubs had agreed to avoid conflicts as long as it went. Though there was war between the clubs. I got hold of the customer and decided time and place. I chose a waypoint at the top of the highway so, it was a public place, so you could avoid shooting. John arrives at the clubyard after 10 minutes saying that he accompanies me and gets me free from this Russian businessman. John said he was driving his bike and he said I would take the car and drive in front of. We brought two handguns as a backup if they had forgotten any kind of trap. This would be the first time I went out with a full member of business. Adrenaline has never pumped on like now. When we arrived, we were almost an hour early. John wanted us to get on the road dinner and eat a little! Eat? I said! I would not be able to get a breadmill if something pushes it down my throat. I was honestly foolish! Though I had my training and a full member with me. Possibly to face a deal in the lower world, nothing was happening and felt awesome in any way. I would love to drive home again! John entered the road dinner and ordered food and then he went to sit at one of the tables, no matter how quiet. There we entered a roadway armed and would eat just before the deal. I only took a glass of water, which was hard enough to get down. John saw that I was loaded and nervous. John was used to this kind of deal. John said that it would not be such a big problem, but that he would take care the negotiations and I just needed to be tightened if it would be a weapon or similar. Certainly! I thought! Just be sharpened, easy when you were like a living milkshake. Of course, I am, I answered John! John told me to get ready after he had eaten. What he said was that I would do a discreet mantle so, I had a cartridge in the race and secure my weapon. Said and done! We started going out of the road. When we got out, there was a nicer car quite far down the car park, and a number of people outside the car. John said there they are! Now I was LOADED!

We are going to John, they said! We started going! They also began to move. But we did not yet know If these were the people we would meet, probably it was! Now we had come so close so, I saw the customer and I tell John that it is them and that I could now see the orderer. Good says John! Now we stood in front of eachother and greeted each other by taking care. The buyer said they would make up an agreement. John ask where it was for a deal? We need that man's services one last time, for a data job. He points at me! John replies that it's not a question and told them to back, now when I belonged to this Mc Club!
The client said that it could mean difficult losses to the club unless they used to use me for a last time for a job. John ask if the customer threaten us. No! said the customer i just say what will happen if they did not use me again one last time. Sorry, John said to the customer! The customer flips a bit. A freak that caused John to explode.

Shit… I thought, it´s banging now, it's banging! I had a real adrenaline kick now! So, I just hoped that I would not let go of my gun. Then I probably could hit the clouds by a drawn weapon. John takes back his right hand behind his back where he had his weapon and told the client one last time to apologize.

The customer understands that we do not negotiate diplomatically anymore. The backup of the client spreads to the sides, now I take my weapon for a while, but do not pull it. I await. The deadlock was what we had right now, somebody's coming out of their car! A man in a long light rock. A very well-behaved person. I understood that that person was the Russian businessman. But it turned out I was wrong. It was the right hand of the Russian businessman. The client began to speak Russian with the person. My Russian language skills were not good at this time, but so much I understood that it was not positive. I watched the Client that he was pushed by the man who recently got off the car and started to speak firmly or in a wiser manner. The customer turns to John and says that his client does not want to let me go without any kind of compensation! John tells the customer that he would be able to offer a bullet in his head if he did not back and the customer apologized. While John says, one of their men goes behind their car and does a mantle. Both John and I pick up our weapons but hold them down to the ground to prevent the public from seeing our weapons. Now it was sharp! The man who was the Russian right hand, says some short words in Russian. Which leads to the customer saying okay okay! We let odd be even says the client. John just changes himself from being a person fully capable of shooting these people to stop his weapon and look happy. I was not happy! I do not know what I was, but I was not happy at all. Everything ends with the customer apologizing and submits his client's wishes once again, get help from me, but they will pay both me and the club. There was nothing I wanted to do. Which John more than knew! John said that our intermediary ends here and now. Which caused the Client and other mourning in that cliff to jump into the car and move away from the parking lot. John says we're going back to the club. Just when we were driving from the parking lot, first

John's searcher dropped and soon my beep was piping. It was the club's phone number! Which meant that you should go straight to the clubhouse immediately. Apparently, something had happened, but what was it? We are wondering if it was the cops that struck again and that we had not been warned by those policemen who were always informed well in advance of a break! We immediately went to the clubhouse to hear or see what had happened. When we entered the yard, some full members came to chat with John. It proved to be a test member who had gone and tattooed in a symbol that only gets if you have the club's consent. But one condition was that you were a full member. Which he was not. Now, this tattoo can sound like a dirt problem. But in the criminal world and especially in the Mc related, the tattoos were very important. Tattoos spoke many languages and each symbol represented what was worthy and had gone through. A very simplified explanation of the importance of tattooing.

John was quite upset and that's the reason they called us back. Full members would advise John on how to resolve this person's unauthorized tattoo.
Everyone agreed that it should go away. The reason no one had seen it was that the guy had a wide leather bracelet on his wrist to just hide the tattoo. But this club owned most of the tattoo studio, and through the tattooist had learned that the guy had requested to get tattooed in this symbol. But even the tattoo artist had been wrong by tapping the symbol when he knew that the guy was not a full member. The tattoo would be at all costs.

And the guy went out into the garage and the grinder with a grinding wheel started.

The guy was in panic but knew that this solution was better punishment than he could get. The angle grinder just wiped away the skin and it flushed skin and blood splash on the walls of the garage. One saw how the blood that hit the walls was sucked into the plasterboard as they hit the plaster wall. There was no one responding. Everyone thought it was right to do that. He had borne a tattoo he could not bear and was now punished. The guy was helped to clean the wound and replace it. The guy would continue his education. The Tatuer was a little bit afraid now, when he knew what the guy got through suffering. The Tatuer got a real warning about what would happen if he did that mistake.

Chapter 29

There was always something that happened at the club and now it was Mirko's trip. He had stuck after an abuse. He received six months in prison for that. Then there was a man short in the middle of the war. But the quota was replenished from Denmark quite quickly. And there were members from other clubs, there was no shortcoming right away. But compared to our enemies or rivals, we were considerably less local. The club started to suspect that those policemen who gave us information about seizures were severely obsessed because they had not been informed for a long time. The club took it safe sooner the uncertainty and move on the weapon store. We started to hide weapons from acquaintances to members who were snowy and were not in the crime register. By hiding large arms stores with ordinary people who had affiliations with someone at the club, the police could not get to the arms. That the prosecutor would request the search of an unstrained person and without evidence was almost unlikely. We could not have any large weapons stores at home. Then the police often hit our home addresses. All tricks are used during the war period. It was very busy. We had no information for several weeks from the police. We could not afford to chances, as it could mean we lost the entire weapon store. It had been a pure disaster.

At the same time, we would train and also keep the order on the market and all territory so no up-knit club tried to claim the club's market shares. All clubs that attempted to enter the market received two choices. Either, it was the members who could drive their club as a sub-club to us and where they had to wear our club colors or liquidation.

Most of the clubs that showed up usually disappeared by solving themselves when they were told we were heading out to their club. There were also the new clubs who wanted to test our capacity and where it went wild. It happened at the end of my trial and there we were going to a new club, to make sure they disappeared once and for all. We had a coach of the rougher model as we jumped into five people. We had the car full of baseball bat, gloves with knogger insulated in the gloves. Someone had a gun with them in case they had firearms! When we reached a crossroads, a policecar slipped alongside us. Do not dare those two snakes to stay us. They went as fast as it became green light. We drove on without their following us.

When we entered the farm where these Mc Guys had hired a part of the farmer's courtyard, the farmer came out with a shotgun. He had the shotgun cartridges in his hand and the rifle was broken. When he saw the West, he entered again. He thought it would be stupid to put his nose into this deal. The guys at this new Mc club were actually quite hazy and had attitude. Which is a good feature of this criminal world! But not against our club. One of our club members! We call him Sam in this book. Sam had a greeting speech that made the most of them back. He had two guns of the brand colt. He began to present himself by firing two shots in the air. But now the whole performance went a little wrong. Sam kept one of the guys in the foot. The guy shouted hysterically of pain when he had a shot in his foot of caliber 45. The bullet went straight through the foot and the bullet stuck in the wooden floor. Now the attention was maximum. All their members say that their club ceases to exist immediately, only we stop shooting them. Their members fly out of the room. Now we went in and broke the place in chips, so they really realized that their club was not welcome on the market. Then we went back to our clubhouse. The second club never seemed to be anymore. This detachment seems to be sure brutal to many! But I can assure you that it was one of the nicer variants.

The fact that our club was exposed to problems every day has probably the most come up to now. But to read about this miserable lifestyle is one thing. Surely many wondering why you continue? You can not stop, even if you would like. You would get into BAD STANDING if you betrayed your brothers and the organization. To leave the club in Good Standing, I personally only feel a case with. But that guy had to buy a loss clubhouse and pay interest and amortization. What was a jump in the million! You can always have good advice and simple solutions when reading this book. But reality is based on many other factors, events and where you are in a more or less brainwashed state. We did many unprotected actions. However, it should be remembered that it took place during an ongoing war. A war like the ordinary population at any particular occasion was affected. But even in war between countries, ordinary innocent people are affected. It was never our intention that these people would be bad, they were simply in the wrong place at the wrong time. The more the war evolved, the greater the resources put into organized crime, the Mc War had a rather extensive budget. The police started pointing out members to psychologically break us. They stood outside the club gate and where they did their utmost with different provocations. For example, they could spit on us or against the drivers and cars driving into the clubhouse. They throw out verbally ugly words. Everything to make us jump on the cop so they could seize us for violence against officials.

When we drove out on our bikes, they were standing there and had traffic check. They had flying inspections on our bikes. They could kick a flasher on the bike, so it was bent, or cleaned out of pieces. Then we were fined for it. Looked so we were sober. Talk to us about people who were in charge of vehicle inspection. So, the police had taken a larger sum from taxpayers who paid this call where the cops broke the law to make us break the law. A nice legal society! The cops stood outside the gates which often had a balaclava over their face, so how tough they really were, could to be discussed. The policemen who warned us had given the impression that there would be a big blow to the clubyard, but it was not the local police force that was supposed to hit, so we did not know when it would happen.

We were quite calm, but, of course, it was tense when the S.W.A.T came. There was a good reason why the colleagues of the police called them for the suicide group. These cops were as trigger-happy as we were. So, when it hit these cops, you never knew what could happen. The club decided that we would be low in business, recovery and other illegal activities for two more days until we saw whether it was successful or not.

We would have a bigger party in the meantime and there would be two professional striptease dancers to celebrate the day for us. Something fun you could have. But our preparedness was at the highest level, which meant that all members could not contribute in this party. Guess if there were protests from those members who would have watched that night. Well then! Count on it…

It would be great food, but we did not directly have someone who could call chef. So, it became potato salad and smoked pork. We dyed with long table and paper-rich, with plastic cutlery. Everybody looked forward to this party. It was the streaks that pulled and made a sigh to party. We had just heard of just one of these stripes. She would be extremely good at her job. We had just begun to eat a bit when the first show started. Everyone stopped eating to see if they were good at stripping. I can say that they were. The main number was the strip that was mentioned. Nobody could eat after her show. She was a very beautiful girl, but her show was purely grotesque. She basically stopped her whole hand in her lower abdomen. It was pure disgusting indeed. No one was directly craving on potato salad after that show. Some even threw their food. She was a bit too rough in her practice when it came to stripping. When we did not even think it was nice, then one could just imagine what ordinary people would like. The party was very good, with many fun elements. We had a human party. Even though the preparedness was at the highest level, we could have a nice time. It felt like those hours that the party lasted, was what made you hurry to take more crap.

Early the following morning, the police force picked up powerfully. We woke up because a chainsaw was running, and it was heard that it looked like something. It would turn out that the Skåne Police Authority had assisted their colleagues in Gothenburg's punching force, and it was now those who made the award. The colleagues had drove down to Skåne because the Prosecutor's Office and the Police Office had made it clear that the Skåne police leaked. The prosecutor was well fed up with all unsuccessful accusations and the state was expensive economically. Not only because they had to replace the club for those inventories that were corrupted by the seizures, but also because the policemen had their salary.

There the prosecutor had to make a well-informed decision on an appeal but without result, which did not look good in the prosecutor's reputation. Where the turnout only became an expensive expense. Thus, the taxpayer's money.

Even this time it became more or less a failure, as they only found smaller things like knuckle-duster and stolen Mc parts. There they could not bind someone to the seizure. The whole turn of events was that a cop team saw a hole in the shelf that surrounded the clubyard and it was the chainsaw that woke up the whole club. Then comes a team of cops in a skylight up against one of the gates at the clubhouse. Two cops who stood in the skylight had its combat helmets wearing tommie-gun as a service weapon. Some members had a hangover, after yesterday's party and wondered where it was happening. The cops throw in both smoke grenades and distraction grenades. It banged like a hell. It was the brightness of the worst New Year's Eve. This time there was a clean war inside the clubhouse. Whenever you look, it was a mess. The cops were disciplined, more than they used to be. They enter the main gate as elite soldiers and where the smallest little moving movement would trigger a shotgun. The cops were very tense, and we were no less active. The cops were worried that we would start to relieve some weapons. But we did not have any weapons there. No more than knuckle-duster and baseball bat. No direct weapon against them. The best thing we could do was let them lock us in once again in the garage, so they could crawl the clubhouse. It started to be a routine routine to have the cheeks in the hedge. That we would not resist was given, when the prosecutor had clapped hands and could lock us in. After the turn it was like the whole farm looked like the city God forgot! Large parts of the plank were destroyed and that was nothing that the police had to pay when they were partially managed by finding theft and illegal weapons. Then the state does not have to pay for the damage, so is the law.

Neighbors to the clubyard found the police to overreact most times. There were high bangs that were called from the distraction grenades, so high that the neighbors stood up in their own beds like fire soldiers. It was children's families and they had to suffer when the police turned off. The police and journalists tended to darken their failure and the journalists only wrote about how effective the organized crime department was, in their efforts to map and eradicate criminal networks. The mass media image of the police's work with great successes lifted to the clouds by those buying journalists whom the police ruled by promising these journalists great storys when other things in society occurred. The police authority would thus give the public a false security picture that the authorities had a full eye on the Mc gang. When the truth is that taxpayers received and still have to pay for the police's failed efforts. Where a portion of taxpayers' income also helped to bend journalists, who would give society a modified image of the effective legal community. A picture of a non-existent civil society.

If the police had been as effective as it was pointed out, many criminals would not be outside prisons and even fewer Mc gangs. But unfortunately, society works in this way. Politicians must provide contributions to the police authority. But no-one has perceived the pingpong game between police and politicians. Because if the police are to get more money, they must show that there is a need. Politicians must see successes in the allocated sums for organized crime.

But there are no successes and does not show the reality that there would be any reduction of the Mc-related organizations, on the contrary. Mc clubs expands too highest for every day. There are subcubes to those big gangs and the big gangs get into new markets. There are currently books in the market that ask why more and more criminal Mc gangs are appearing right now. Truth is not as sophisticated as you can imagine.

The basic life requirements a high occupant had. Be Brotherhood, be free, out of law, take care of yourself and the business that you undertook. That the war starts is easy to explain when the market in this country is limited, and there, market shares were the very foundation of the war. Again, I would release their market shares to the other club. That's a conflict! WAR…

Driving power in the war became cash, money! Difficult, you do not need to explain it. But solving it was much more difficult. When two strong clubs fight for the same cake it becomes a mess. Just like in normal life, nothing strange in it. The problem was that Mc Gang did not dedicate himself to anything and that is what is different from the rest of society. Where those elected citizens follow the law book and have human barriers. These barriers can only be fired through a hard life.

Chapter 30

This club had to create safe income for the fixed expenses. The club initially had major income from drugs, recoveries, taking over tattoo studios. This step also called the first wave! The word WAWE, would come to be the word that described the criminal development for the public. The second wave consisted of sheltered activities by restaurants and other companies, where these companies had no major choice if they needed this protection or not. They would have this protection. Otherwise, their company could disappear in the signs of the flags and the holder of the restaurant could wake up at MAS, Malmö General Hospital. This was pure extortion at the high level. A mandatory protection that would be paid by the percentage of annual turnover for such a company. The second wave also consisted of many other parts, such as prostitution and human trafficking. But where the contact was not directly connected to the Mc Club but managed by other people who stood directly under our club. Many believed that the full members were the worst, but that was exactly the opposite, when full members did not shit their hands unnecessarily. As mentioned, the dirt was done by the dogs. Those energetic dogs who wanted to enter the club had absolutely no barriers. They would turn out to be skilled and many times they were used to their aspirations, becoming a full member.
Where many became very disappointed when they were only used to the utmost.

But one of the sources of income used was collided with the club's own philosophy! About how to care for their women with respect. At the same time as income escalated from prostitution, where the basic body consisted of women. Certainly, this source of income was very far out in the branch of the network itself. But it does not matter, it's a principle discipline. The authorities did their utmost to get into the organization through Undercover's operations. Where police tried to sneak in. Which judgment really succeeded in the second gang we were in war with. That the police came in there were due to their way of recruiting new members. By planting policemen in the Mc Clubs, they would try to predict the next step in the criminal wave. But the third wave could not predict authorities. And it was through this desperate attempt that would give authorities a head, start to turn on before the organization struck back on society's legal system. But the authorities expect the wrong return fire. Where authorities believed that Mc's gang would get a strong position through threats and other illegalities. Probably the movie is THIRD WAVE! What best describes what would happen, but the movie came first 10 years later. Then society was already defenseless and there the information was function-free. It was the third wave that made all the authorities completely upset. There is no protection against the third wave.

For the authorities, focus on grabbing criminals in different criminal organizations and losing total grip on what it really was about. Money is Power!

The club confused the authorities by attracting their attention to the wrong establishment areas, thereby making it possible for the big savings bank to be vigorously filled. Through the organization's large capital at different banks abroad, the first phase of the third wave could begin to take shape. The club began to take over various companies in a completely legal manner. By buying up the company's shares. That any company would sell 51 percent, so the club got a share majority! And, thus, could control the company in the direction desired. Those companies who refused became easy to persuade, as they would only have peace and quiet. There was always a businessman who would play Brother Good! But they do not exist in this country anymore. The club always calculated with a certain loss of both money and members. That was the price of success. A price that not even a Mc club could avoid. The losses that often hit the club were that someone went to prison. An acceptable loss when companies were in the club's interests.

The club always pay for the shares, so at that point it was not illegal. But just when you'd get them 51 percent who gave a leading position in the business! It was usually quite strange, and with a lot of unlawful threats and violence! The club had decided, then it just became! In one way or the other! But the company should enter the club's organization as well as network. But our club was not the only one who had these plans, and the acquisition of different companies became the pure hardware that was worth the gold in double sense. By collecting those companies' liquid assets, they could be used for establishment and development. But also, to get illegal items, such as liquor, drugs and weapons. Most often, the acquired companies had a very good reputation, which made it much easier to collect those illegal goods! Those entrepreneurs would definitely not get together with the club. And even less, they wanted customs and police to detect their assistance to crime. That fear made it easy to keep calm and carry out, for example, transportation.

Though they might have done anything to escape. Everything was very carefully planned by the club. Where every company became a puzzle in the organized work. Being able to utilize these entrepreneurs created amazing opportunities at an international level. Where the club's other brothers in other countries could easily send important equipment. No one could imagine that a reputable company drove gun transport. But so was the reality! A reality that passed the common citizen. Many of the corporate executives bought by the club were allowed to live a double life against their own families. Where they kindly kept the color and there, they no longer had control over their own company. A terrible fate for those people, where they could only make a police report. But then their lives would be, either very short, or become a life that would make the hell perceive the purity of heaven. Very few people police detect a Mc club. Those who reported! Undo today! Certainly ...

But back to the event ...

A lot of violence was required on certain occasions when the club tried to buy the companies. Such kind of violence as few People can perform without being affected or mentally injured. Mirko was such a person who had an extreme mood and did not suffer at all to harm other people in whatever condition he was. Mirko was supposed to released from his prison sentence for 6 months offense and all the clubs had high expectations of his mood's resources would be of great benefit during the third wave. A number of members had prepared Mirkos released with a party and some nice girls, as girls do not grow directly on trees before the prison walls. But soon it would appear that Mirko would not get out of the box. There had been a murder in prison where Mirko was sitting. The case was that Mirko had learned, that one of

the interns had leaked Information to the guards in prison
about an incident and where the person who was revealed
was placed on the insulation. A tattle that made Mirko
crazy. Mirko then takes one of his own socks and puts in
two billiard balls. Then he walks in to the guy in his cell,
who tattle his companion and sat on the insulation. He
gives a pair of bangs in his head and then finish by hit the
sock with the billiard balls a number of times in the head
of the guy. Which causes the guy to get his forehead
depressed and it causes a serious internal bleeding. Then
Mirko puts the guy in bed and draws the blanket over the
head of the boy like pissed blood. Then he again pulls the
cell door and leaves from there.

When the guard would then lock the interns, the guard say
good night and usually the good-night person says
goodnight too. But not in this case. The guy is
unconscious under the blanket and can not immediately
say anything. The guard then believes that the guy already
sleeps, and just closes the cell door again. In the morning
when the guard opened the cell door, they realized that a
serious crime had occurred. The guy had died during the
night of their internal injuries. Had the guard just entered
the cell in the evening, the life of the boy could have been
saved, according to the investigation made at the prison.
The alarm went and the guard began to scan the cells
according to Mirko's data. They found the sock that
proved that Mirko had carried out the assassination
attempt according to the technical evidence provided by
the police during the investigation itself. The prosecutor
charged Mirko with points of action, such as assassination
alternatively homicide.It ended with homicide attempts
after all negotiations. Where Mirko got six years in
prison. He never came back to the club.

Despite the great loss of a member, the war continued as nothing had happened! It just got worse for every day that went. Now it was war on the highest level. Where we had directives like giving the opponents the motto that we so hardly observed.

The opponent would blow up in the air once and for all. Dan… our weapon expert and some other members planned an operation against our enemies. It would be an operation that would write history in this war. Dan, considered that a bazooka of the brand Carl Gustav. With a shot of 84 mm would do the job thoroughly. Everyone thought that this shot would blow up our enemies' entire clubhouse and all those who were inside that building. The planning was rigorous on this particular operation. Properly planned, this could mean a local victory and a larger market area. Which basically was about. Said and done! A group climbs on a roof about 150 meters from the club's local area, and begins to rig up the bazookan and charges the armor. Everyone was crazy about the effect that the bazooka shot would have at their clubhouse. Dan was the only one who could handle the bazookan and it was therefore forced for him to shoot. Dan is shooting away the armor shot, it became sound that corresponds to 50 new year missiles being shot away. They 150 meters as the armor was supposed to be known as an eternity. The shot hits in their woods and goes straight through the whole house and out on the other side to land in the grass. We saw everyone surprised when we had expected an explosion. It was an explosion that did not seem to exist. Everybody looks now on Dan! What the hell happened? Was the first spontaneous question that appeared in our minds? I do not know said Dan!

What? Do you not know? No something has gone wrong! Do you believe that we said! No, how the hell can you believe it? At the same time, we quickly climb down the ladder again and went away with the car that took us to this place. It was a damn life in the car and where we now began to wonder and question Dance skills on a bazooka, we could not go to our clubhouse, when the cops would start looking there and now, we have hot potatoes. We had arranged a safehouse and it was now where we went. Everyone was mad at Dan when this operation was totally unsuccessful. When we arrived at the house we were going to stay for a few days, discussions began to go high. Then we would keep our jaws closed as he wondered what went wrong. When he thought for a while, he realized that it had been a gun-armed shot and that was exactly what was the fault. The shot hit the wooden board, and such a shot must hit a concrete or steel sheet material to explode. What flop that operation became, not only because the shot did not explode, but also because their full members were not in the room. There was only one of their sample members in the room and he sat watching television when the shot went across his head and out through the other end. The test member must be quite loose in the stomach when a bazooka shot draws through the TV room.

The police were now crazy for the perpetrators, who shot a bazooka shot. It is very serious to carry out such surgery. Fortunately, no one was injured, but it could have devastating consequences if the shot had exploded. There maybe all their members had died. But there was nothing you thought about then, it's only now that you realize the madness of this action. It was war and harmlessness to the enemy was the only thing that was relevant at that time.

Chapter 31

Our enemy, of course, saw this action as a very serious escalation of the war, and they were not late to bring countermeasures. Already the day after the Bazooka shot, plant them a hand grenade in one of our cars, under the hood. They must be extremely stressed when they mount your hand grenade. Firstly, they did not get the whole hood back, which was probably a strategic plan. Then they had put a steel wire in the ring itself that made it possible to pull out the sprint. The steel wire had them tied into the hood itself. So their intention was to lift the hood and then the steel wire would pull out the sprint and the hand grenade would explode. This could work if they did not put too long a wire. This hand grenade could easily be removed and secured. This was just the beginning of the escalation of a very cruel and long war, between two Mc gang. All of these planted hand grenades and other explosives, put pressure on the police authority. Who was often assigned to go out to PULLING DOORS as they called it. Pulling doors meant that the police had to tie a string around the door handle and then back a number of meters, then pulling the door in order to see it slammed. All who were involved in this war became scary. It appeared in many different ways. But our organization got inverted and where we treat everyone more or less like the worst enemy, which makes you see everything in black. You could only trust your brothers, nobody else. You developed a mechanical part on your own body purely mentally for each day that went. Whilst this sick mood developed with me as a person, I had two children to take care of each other weekend. Anna realized that I was out on extremely thin ice and started action against me. She began to want the custody of our common children. Which became another pure warfare! Although it was the best she did, I could not accept this humiliation for my life. I could not see my own children's best. The children were mine. But I did not see my own ill-treating steps in crime's bottom lame. It felt like one was just set on a frequency that was just about destroying, crushing and liquidating. No normal feelings could penetrate firmly in the middle, more than well, knew that one was not like a person. One was controlled by a remote control and was centrally controlled by the organization's evil center. At the same time, feeling an unprecedented power and lack of feeling. Feelings are probably the hardest one can describe in a credible way, but these words above are so close you can get the feelings register I had at that time.

Finally, I realized that the best for the children was that Anna had custody and wrote the papers her legal representative had compiled. At that time, I had begun to realize how wrong I was about it and through my signature did something good during this gloomy time. Anna and my friendship relationship were not very well said. But we could in any case be in the same room without any major conflicts.

But realizing that making mistakes is one thing, doing something about it is a completely different matter. Something just a few hours after the signature was gone, and there, as a person, I thought that they thought they had only been a temporary confusion. The war and the club once again took a strength of both me and my thoughts. I was soon back on track and fully active in the criminal little world in which you lived. Like everyone else in the club, I was determined to beat our enemies. Indeed, they had realized the knowledge of the third wall and where there were many advantages, but not least large liquid assets that could easily be managed by those who took them first. Our next move was to throw in a number of hand grenades before their plank and there hopes that this Mc Gang would disappear from the area of pure fear, as a rain of hand grenades can make anyone be easy on the soles of the feet and fast. The plan was to get behind their clubhouse. At the back of their farm there was a small stream. It was on the spring edge and quite chilly yet in the evenings. We only had a few meters before we were so far ahead that we could throw in the hand grenades. After these hand grenades collapsed, the plan was to enter their headquarters and rig some real explosives, so the entire building would be tiled. But some members of their gang appeared on the back as they would pee and see us. Now it was fireworks. Everybody emptied their magazine by the occurrence of such a shooting. It bangs like hell. I was completely sleepy and just kidding on the ground was completely natural. Forget all you watched movies, where the hero stands up and shoots. This was a sharp place with shielded weapons and as guaranteed, all of the site became completely hyperactive. I felt that an overdose of adrenaline. I just felt the finger of the trigger that just pressed and pressed until the cartridges were over. In principle, the sound of the weapons was not heard, although there were noise levels that could cause them to die without any problems. No one was prepared for this development. We had to go back when our enemies had about 36 men, in the club and we were only 7 men, at the moment. We would have been slaughtered at least if we stuck there. When we go back, the member Sam attached, being ill and unable to move. He was not injured, but if he touched, they had seen him. And then they would probably have executed him on the spot. We could not go back immediately, as it would probably lead to more shooting. Sam had probably ended the ammunition and if we had gone back, he would probably not have been able to defend himself. We did not dare to risk this. It was decided that we should wait a few hours. Sam had crashed into the pelvis as it fluttered anything but hot water. The pause that was thought for a few hours would soon be almost two days. We did not know if Sam would fix for two days in cold water. Not for it was winter, but probably cold enough to get sick. After almost two whole days we got a position, so we could pick up Sam!

He was barely aware of the cold water. Two men had picked him up and took him to our clubhouse. He was in great need of care. He had to be taken to the nearest hospital as he had taken double-sided pneumonia and had high fever because of this.

Now there were two men less and things did not make things easier. It started rolling in members from Denmark, so the quota would be held. I was so tired, so you almost saw stars, but had to go on. My mood was like an ECG that went up and down. I lit on all cylinders for sketches. Everyone was as tired. I just wanted to lay down. The tiredness was probably a lot of psychic, when I was involved in things that few people need to experience and which I do not want anyone to experience, even in their worst nightmares.

We decided to visit the house where this club was once formed. We went to the old clubhouse and try to relax, if only for a few hours. Someone had a smaller party and we were invited so it felt okay to go there. There were spirits, partygirls and other nice people. A lot of ordinary people came to the party.

Many thinks that life we were living was very interesting. Many who wanted to feel free, but they could not, because, first of all, they did not have a psyche for such a life. But also, because they had their families to take care of.

The girls cluster around us just we got there and were so nice so. But I grew up with brides and their curiosity quite soon. They just wanted to be seen and did anything to get there and sit on our bikes. But we had our view of women and now, after all, I think that view was a bit shabby. Not because we should beat a woman or make them ill purely psychologically. But while letting them strip, feel a little opolitically, with double messages. During the party, people came to us and said that there was a guy in the party who was boasted that he used to stay outside the plank of the clubhouse and aim on us with laser sight. We only had to check if it was really true that someone would be so suicidal that the person went and said such things. Or if it was just an ammunition or perhaps a bad assault. The guy was quite hard to find out it was a smaller party. We walked inside the party and just wished we should hear this guy brag about his braves against club members. A girl appears and points out the guy. We go and stand three men behind his back to hear if he really spoke and talked shit. We could quickly find out that the guy was affected by spirits and was full of saying things like. **Quote**: Mc guys are totally harmless I could shoot them easily without even noticeing where the shots came from. I have a laser look and usually hold the red dot in their heads. **End quote.**

I knocked the guy on his shoulder, then Dan took one step forward! What was the name of the Mc gang saying Dan, the guy soaked in a millisecond and began to stutter, their name is Red Bulls, I believe! said the guy. Dan asked the guy if it´s not a softdrink for little guys like him, and also said he did not know a Mc gang in these regions with that name. The guy laughed very uncertainly and hoped there would be no problem. Dan told him he would accompany us to the clubhouse. The guy tried to get out of the place, but he did not succeed. Dan told him to go on his HD with him to the club, so he could see if it was our plank that the guy ran around with a laser aiming. We had to tie the guy around Dan! So, he would not jump off on the go.

Once again at the club, the boy started to get a free kick, as he now understood that he would get strength because he had gone crazy. We pulled him into the clubhouse, put him in a chair and tied him with silver tape. Dan Just wanted to scare the guy. We had no intention of harming him, but there to scare him so he stopped running and talking that he was aiming at us with laser sight during the prevailing War. Dan says that he was back soon! I thought that's coming now, he put in a weapon to scare him. No weapon but there against a chainsaw. Oh! I thought in my quiet mind. The guy shouts hysterically when Dan tells him he's going to live but, wanted to cut him off the leg so we'd be late. I knew Dan would not do anything so damn stupid. But that did not know the guy. Dan! Starting the chainsaw and gases on quite a lot, the whole room was smoked with two-stroke mixed gasoline. Now the guy kept popping off. Dan adds the chainsaw chain to the boy's jeans, so much so that your jeans slip. The guy both pissed and fell down in total. It stinks too damn! We had to cut the tape and have life in the guy. He nodded and ran very quickly out of the clubhouse and did not stay on the nearest stretch. That guy never even talks more.

Yes! Violence was frequent, and it took me very psychologically when I as a person never wanted to hurt people. In order to cope with this misery, I began to drink large amounts of Whiskey. I was not for drugs in any way. But alcohol is also in large amounts a big problem like any drug.

An addiction that amounted to 8 bottles or more per week when it was the worst. That I drank so much is because I can not handle this amount of violence without any kind of anesthetic. I really did not want to carry on violence or hurt people. I only had dollars as the foundation of my crime and now had a solid list of a lot of crimes. All you did was criminal, whatever you did, it was connected or was a pure criminal act.

I was quite far from my safe hacker world. Now it was about filling their quota against the club and even earning dollars

Chapter 32

It was decided that I would be responsible for a larger delivery of stolen cars of the more luxurious variant and where they would have new paint and new signs. Thus, a stolen car should be legal. I had a successful delivery of 20 cars. It was often so if one succeeded, one would repeat the same approach again. It was something I personally protest many times in return. The risk of doing that was that it became a pattern that the police could analyze and follow up. Not to mention a nasty prosecutor would get facts on the table if you were to fail.

I had met the person who took the cars in the country a number of times and he seemed quite alright! But this time I went on a blow. A blow that was costing me life. Kenna and John were well aware of this deal. There would be big gains in a successful business. A million-dollar win. Which meant that many would get their part. Last time I met the person who took in the vehicles in the country, he left a list of all registration numbers. The first thing I did was check the registration numbers against the car registration database, so these numbers were not already there. If they had been there, it would have been a scam. But all of them were registred and that was positive.

I was talking to Kenna and John! What did they think about the deal? Not because we had paid a few dollars in advance. But contacting people like the club did business with in the usual case was a big risk if it proved to be a big scam. It became high-level games, where the club's rush would be shameful unless the deal was completed.

John thought It was worth checking out an extra time, so everything was okay with the cars and that they really existed. What I did by requesting a chat with the contact person, who had the cars in Germany. The information I received was a company name with a real organization number and where all these papers were okay with the authorities. So that was so true. Even those registration numbers that were on the list, the German guy could confirm. But the guy also left the correct dates on the delivery days. I was dubious when many of the cars would go to the club's customers who were highly regarded. The club could not do bad business, as we always kept our word, no matter what it would be like, a word was holy and never broke.

I decided to complete the deal and gave my contact a clear sign. The guy said that the cars will come quite fast from ordering them, and that they would check the vehicles, which is a requirement for imported vehicles. I would only make sure to distribute the vehicles to those new owners and to be in control of it. The cars would arrive in Halmstad and from there I would arrange to come to Helsingborg in an industrial area on Berga! The same day as the first car-delivery was to be done, the guy called and told us that there was one day delivery delay! Due to lack of space I started to get bad vibes! Which was the worst thing that could happen! I immediately took an extremely aggressive attitude towards the guy. I explain directly, that if there was wrong on this buisness, he was damn badly out there! A message that the guy really took care of seriously. I called John! Because I wanted to meet him, to tell he about the delay. John got everything else a happy one on that guy and would probably lower him directly, without the slightest hesitation. John's spontaneous comment was that he should manage their Commitments Otherwise, a whole new group will be linked to that guy. John tells me that one of the customers who ordered a majority of these cars, could cause problems since they were anything but harmless. The pressure on me was not immediately diminished because I had to get this deal in port so, the club's reputation would not be ashamed in any way. Now it had been a day and it was time for delivery, but no cars came! I began to see that this deal would contain a lot of unpleasant violence. I understood that now I had to find that guy who did not manage his business and that quickly.

Impressions and a lot of requests from the club's big customer had already begun on the first day. But those questions had John answered and did not tell me anything! When he did not think I would feel better knowing that there was a hard pressure against the club, then the cars were not delivered. Kenna calls me on the phone! And want me to come home to him. When I entered Kennas apartment he told me that I would keep a very low profile when the big customer wanted to get me. I tell Kenna that I take care of the guy himself! And telling he, I look him up. Kenna did not want me to go, as there were great risks of having me out there and when there were people in the lower world who was looking for me intensively. But I had decided! So, I went to Halmstad to the street address mentioned by the guy at our first meetings. When I arrived, there was no person at the name I was looking for. I could not get into my head that somebody would dare to mess up with the club. It was pure suicide, to do such a thing.

After a lot of searching, I find the boy's brother who was strangely said dark afraid when I arrived, looking for his brother.

He tells that his brother left the country two days ago but did not know where to go! He would not have liked to tell his brother when this brother could reveal the destination if he should be pressed. I realized that I had to sort out this deal in some way.

Called John and Kenna and tell me how it was! They said we would meet halfway in the morning and that I had to look for threads that could lead to the actual perpetrator until then. I was looking for everything, and I was extremely angry and violent against everyone I would get out of information. Because I would have got it or those people who thought it was possible to trick me out. I was completely obsessed with your guilt so, it went quite dramatically, with much violence. It was hard to figure out who to hang in the toes! For this failure and the issue that was of increasing importance, was who made an economic profit on this bluff business?

I drove into a gasoline tank to refuel and find something edible. I was totally upset that I was hungry in the pursuit of these perpetrators, who put me in a very difficult situation. Once inside the mack, it turned out they did not have anything that attracted a hungry Swedish belly. There was a restaurant adjacent to the gasstation and I went in to order a real blowout meal. When I went into the restaurant, I saw those people who were looking for me. It got right in the middle of the door and quickly turned around to go out of the restaurant. But I just got to the sliding doors so some of their gangs came to me from the outside. Absolutely amazing what the world is small. But they had been in the same area to look after me as well as the guy I was looking for. Of a clean reaction, I tried to get away from the place, but they were two, I bet hard and hit my elbow straight on the one's nostrils, which is broken directly, and the blood just splashes, and his eyes begin to drain. What was the idea of that battle! Then it would just be one of the guys left. But Those who sat in the restaurant came running to their help, and it became impossible for me to get rid of me. They are pulling me into a car and put me in the back seat and a gorilla on each side of me! So I could not take me out of the car.

Chapter 33

Then they drive me to an apartment and begin to hear and abuse me by tapping a baseboll tree in my head on my left side so the eyebrow is cracking. A bang that waves me pretty well! The whole room was spinning and I could not see anymore, because it ran into my eye. Then I get repeated bangs against my body and against my left elbow. What was such a hard bang, so it looked like it hung a bowling ball under my elbow as it swelled up. It made the real damn pain! Which meant I just wanted to kill that guy! But there was a guy, beside the guy who hit me, with a big damn knife that had a knife blade of almost 30 cm. So it was not a good location right now.

One of the guys comes up to hear if I wanted to tell you where the cars were gone! And who had been pretty close to sneaking the cars? I said to that guy! That he would call John at the club because he could certify who I was. The guy in the baseball tree, beats me to my left shoulder, and half screaming I'm just talk crazy! But the guy who came up to ask the questions, know who John at the club was and wanted to get John's phone number. I gave him the number so he could call John!

Meanwhile, the guy with the baseball tree begins to get a much more insecure appearance. He was, very worried that it was the truth I said at first! He looked at it all the time The person who talks with John on mobile phone. After a few minutes, the call ends. The guy with the baseball tree asks directly if I was the person I issued to be? Well, he is, answer the guy like ring John! The guy with the baseball tree just drop the baseball tree straight down on the floor. He understood that he was a very dead man! When he completely broke me halfway.

John and Kenna would come to the place where I was caught and beaten. Meanwhile, we waited for them to pop up! I ask for some spirits, to die the pains that were powerful. My head dunk like Big Ben was inside the head. They had 80 percent Rome! As I got a bottle of. That was fine! I drew a number of glasses of this Rome so I would feel a bit better. I do not know which one did the most pain, the head or the elbow. But what was most difficult was the blood that siped out of the temple and ran into the eye. I had to hold my shirt against the open wound, so the blood would stop. But it was not easy to stop it. When Kenna entered the room with John, did he get a oblique ignition when he saw how I looked! Kenna was great as a house, and now he was crazy. He lacks one person after another! So they would think they were beaten on the wrong person. Kenna holds the guy, with the baseball tree in the shirt, and give him two really hard bangs in the middle of the face. The guy drops when his knee folds. He was, extinguished for a few seconds. Not strange with two bangs of a person who practices 150 kg in bench press in normal cases. There was pressure behind the battles that the guy had received.

Kenna wondered what I wanted to do with the guy! And also ask how many bets I had received from him? Something that was not straightforward was easy to remember! Then, at least, I was angry with the 80 percent rome that had begun act! Kenna thought I would cut a finger for each kind. I got up from the couch! It was spinning pretty well in my head after the treatment I had received. John would I want to get closer to him when he wanted to say something a bit discreet.

John said I would imagine what decision I took when it
came to the guy who was abusing me. The reason was
that there were a number of people outside the club who
had been involved in this detention! And it made it totally
impossible to remove the guy from the earth's surface.
Even though I was mad enough and crazy about that guy,
I could not do anything, that way at least. I was very
hateful to the guy and I really wanted to beat the shit out
of him. I got up the guy so, he got up on his legs. I gave
him a really fat bang, which hit under his eye and the skin
burst just under the eye. It started to drain blood from the
guy! And I really felt I could kill him! The guy apologizes
and says it was a big mistake, what happened. That was
probably the only one we agreed. I just let go of the guy
and told him! That our ways never crossed more! Because
then I promise! That it has a completely different
outcome. The guy had to leave the apartment severely
injured. I have never been so sure that it would be right to
kill someone! But I'm relieved that I took my common
sense to catch and did not do more with the guy. Kenna
thought the guy was too shy away.
Two days later, it was time to have the children. I would
pick them up at Anna's home.

Chapter 34

When I ring the door! Opens Anna and see how I look.
Probably not a beautiful sight. I had a bulb of 2-3 cm high
which sat over my left eye and my left eye was
completely painted with all the colors of the rainbow.
Under that bump I had an open wound, which look
anything but good. Anna immediately said that the
children could not

come to me! As long as I looked like I did. Something
that made me light up slightly. Now afterwards, her
decision was a very wise decision. But in the present
hour, it was just an anger I knew about Anna. I was kind
enough to go away without the kids, to go home and lick
the wounds as it is called. John knew that I would be
home a few days after this abuse, which I have been
exposed to! And it felt nice to just relax without a lot of
must. We had decided that this car shop would be done
thoroughly, as soon as I was a bit better. It took a lot
longer to recover, than I had previously thought. Maybe
not so strange! It was a damn mass of kind that I received!
And that had hurt me quite a lot! But after the rain comes
the sunshine! I started after a week to open my left eye
again, even though it was blurred, what I saw! Did it feel
pretty anyway! It was painful and my body sore in many
places. My elbow got a big bang and felt after more than
one week more or less abusive. I thought it had the
swelling to do and that just that swelling pushed on a
nerve. But I can tell after 10 years I still have numbness in
that arm.
That's how it costs to be on top. A peak I wish I had never
reached. But now it was only to realize that it was late and
make the most of the worst!

Eight days after the mishap, it was time to look for the sins. Although we knew it would be extremely difficult, I was determined to find them. For them they had a great blame pay, but also my own anger against the responsible, created a driving force that was called! I'd just beat the shit out of the guy! Even if I saw, there would be a risk of getting caught. But that guy would only be lowered. The thoughts I had before I became beaten began to appear again. It was the thought of who would be so damn suicide suspects that it would risk getting a whole organization in the hedge of the small sums it was about. You do not fool such an organization at 1-2 million kronor and think that they could stay away throughout their lives! It would not be that sum of money enough. It was only after I thought about these thoughts for a while, as I started to understand that the guy I had had contact with, Probably yourself had been snuffed on the confection! At the same time, I wondered why the guy had not told me anything, so we could give him backup. I had just give him the warning, if there were problem in the buisness. But so seriously I did not think that the warning was, so the guy could not ask for help. But maybe my warning had scared him too much, so he might feel better to leave the country. Just leaving the country with the knowledge of never returning requires a big planning, or he would have been pressured by the German car dealer? And be scared of his guard? Yes! The questions were many, but the answers shone with their absence.

I called John and wondered if there was any success, a little coded and discreet. John just replied that the organization's, German club had found the company and would go out to get hold of the company sign and shake him strongly, so we could get clarity in this deal. This tells John with completely different words. I said I went to relatives again. Then to the boy's brother who had contact with me! To hear and pump this on data. The brother was not home, so I waited half an hour then his brother was an ordinary Smith who worked in the days. When the brother arrives at his home, I leave the car. The brother sees me and becomes very nervous! But does not run in. He stands and waits until I arrive at him. The brother began to tell me before I even said hello! That his brother had sent two boxes with BMW's keyrings that lay in a similar box as a plain socket wrench kit. In those plastic boxes, all the keys were in all series, so we could start all the cars. The keys did not look like common keys. They looked like a mandrel that you notice iron or metal pieces! And at the bottom of this mandrel-like item was a key. You should simply drive the key in the ignition switch, and then use an ordinary 10 mm wrench to turn the ignition off so the car starts. A pretty smart construction that really worked! The problem was just that we did not have the cars. So, the question that appeared in the head was what we should have the new words to. Either it was the guys explanation that he kept his part, and himself had been blown or it was a mocking laugh.

John had some major successes from the German side. They had got hold of the owner, of the company who would deliver the cars. He did not believe in his worst nightmare that he had fooled a Mc gang and had therefore stayed in his native country.

It turned out that the car dealer had driven this blow to many groupings, but our organization was among those few clients who did not pay in advance. But our words had become shameful. Perhaps not so obvious, but it was bad enough, when we always kept our word in a deal.

Of course, someone would pay for the damage, even if it did not have an economic injury, it would have been a bad reputation for the club. Which could not be accepted under any circumstances. The whole deal ends with our club taking over the German car company, then company signer gets a half a million bet. The club was then compensated for the big customer with a few hundred thousand, so that business relationship would not go into the run. Everyone was not as happy about the outcome of this deal. It was the German car dealer who made one last desperate attempt to keep his company. This German car dealer threatens the German local Mc Club in our organization by sending Maffian to the club If he did not return his business. There were many who had difficulty quitting when the club arrived. But the German car dealer thought he had scared the club. He goes so far that he travels to Sweden to make up the deal. A deal that was already ready from the club. To jump at the club must be a crazy work. What this German car dealer got to know? He went out into an old barn. This barn was the actual meeting point and where the German car dealer would bring his bodyguards. There were some clever bodyguards, then they jumped and hid then the noice of some shots in the air. The German car dealer was severely battered in that barn. Probably all the bones were broken, and a member joins the German car dealer and tells him how badly he is at him, and in the meantime, he tells the German car dealer what he likes, Up a injection needle and a pump that he usually had to pump testosterone and other doping preparations when he was training. But this time he would make a point for this fool! As he shouted once and for all. I wondered what he would do. This member went out to his bike, took off the gas cap and sucked the whole pump with gasoline. Then he goes in with the syringe and pulls the needle into the throat of the German car dealer! And tell him! If you wont, get back to your damn Hitlerland immediately! Will you get clean petrol straight into your throat.

We others who were in the barn ran against this member and threw us over him, so he would not push the gasoline into his throat. Then it would mean that man died immediately. The car dealer began hyperventilating when he realized that his life was in great danger. He no longer had any problems with the fact that this Mc Club owned his company and that he had a debt of half a million at the same time. The guy I had had contact with received a message from us, Through his brother! That he could come home to his family again. Then, apparently, he was not trying to blow us. When the German car company went through thoroughly, all the information was found on which registration numbers the German car dealer had used! But also, what groups he had tried to blow the confection. Because this Mc Club now owned the car company, the club was forced to blow off all these blowing attempts. What everyone involved was thought very well and they could get back their efforts ... in part! The club's expenses were deducted first.

At the same time, I had made a frog in the store! Then it ended happily for my part and I got a good impression that I was doing my business. This deal ended with significantly higher profit margins than the club first calculated. But it was not straightforward, and it was not a business that went into diplomacy. I myself had been seriously injured and there are still days of this affair in my life.

The deal became like a well-adapted puzzle piece in the third wave, although it was initially thought of as a financial supplement to the clubhouse. That's a successful but painful deal.

I can now think that the third wave was the most violent of all of them. Though it was the third wave that would make the illegal legally. That there were high discussions when someone tries to take over the decisive share in a company is quite understandable. But that so many people just dared to risk their own lives actually amaze me. Then it's about money and real estate at all. But many times, the company was well-founded. Of course, you are defending such a thing. But not at any price. I was now a person with a tolerance far beyond humanity! And where I was hard as granite, I became like a human or more like a machine, harder for every day. My psyche tolerated almost anything! And as a parable with a construction worker who gets calluses in their hands, the more they work, just as well became my psyche for everything that I agreed. The big difference is that an injured psyche or an exposed psyche lets you carry the rest of your life. While a professional's calluses disappear with time.

In connection with a loud night! Stop the club outside of a nightclub. It was quite messy outside. It got calmer when we arrived. The funny thing about this occasion was that our nemesis stood at another night club across the road. When we had stayed, they called us and wave that we would come over! So, they could invite us to a beer. Sure, life is strange! And our life was strange! One week we tried to kill each other or blow each other. For a week later to invite and drink beer together ... Comment unnecessary! We did not drink beer with our enemies, it would not look so good. We remained on our side. Rather soon, there will be a pretty big guy to Sam and start touch at his bike, which was a death sin and Sam marked straight away so the guy would assume that you do not touch the bike without law! The guy completely wacked what Sam said! Probably it was becuse great intoxication. Sam get really angry and, warn the guy and tell him to get off the bike immediately. What the guy did! But Sam, as was now really pissed off and pick up a knuckle-duster with welded small knife blades that were about 1.5 cm long and start knocking the blades into the breast's chest. The guy got 2-3 knife sticks! Sam, Saying ice cold to the guy! You bleed the boy! Believe you have to go to a hospital ... so it was the quiet moment! We had to return to the clubhouse. The police came out soon at the clubyard to find the perpetrator. The suspect had left a signal that was similar to Mirko! But these policemen were not updated. Had they checked Mirko before, they knew that he was sitting at an institution, which is the world's best alibi. So, the police tried to find someone like that. We asked them to go to hell! Then they had no search. Which made these cops quite awful! But we had the law on our side, and they knew that very well.

The difference between criminals' business and the usual business community is not as huge as you might think! Certainly, we had no limitations and there were often stolen things that were sold on. But by the way, a good business deal went smoothly and sensibly, as long as no one tried to blow us in one way or another.

A business deal could take place in a restaurant like in the ordinary business community. However, there were big differences if something went wrong! Or if someone walks into one's territory.

What could happen to you for a business dinner one day, and the second day it was war! Where you tried to kill the other partner. This event was not too unusual and if a debt was not paid on time, hardly a collection notice of 150 SEK was added as an additional cost. No! Then it was about giving that person clear and clear rules of conduct and in the worst case it ended with a weapon grease in the forehead.

Life was very hard and you would always be on guard. Everyone who was new at the club wondered when they were going to put on the vest and how long it took before they got their full membership. But it was a question that was never answered, so someone could understand what it meant to become a full member. The answers given were that when that day comes! Do not you know if you're going to laugh or cry. That was the only answer given. On the day it would be celebrated that a person became a member, the person in question really noticed. There were some different member reviews. One of these rituals was to take out the person in a forest when the club was riding a bike. To later stay and go out into the woods to grill and party as it was so hot. Now it was not any party without the celebration of a new full member.

The event was that all those involved went into the woods at a planned location and when we were almost at the woods a number of weapons, such as Ak4 and other small arms, were drawn and directed at the person who would become a full member. Then this person gets farther into the woods to soon see an excavated hole in the ground. The person in question is relying on pure fear and confusion. The thoughts are spinning! The person is wondering what this has done to be subjected to a resignation. When then The guy is in front of the dug hole in the ground, this is said to turn against the cliff. As now shooting off the entire magazine. It smells so deep into the hell and the person falls down on the ground of pure shock. It is only loose ammunition in the weapons that are being relieved. Then after the magazine is over, everyone runs to the person and congratulates this and welcomes as a full member of the club. After such a celebration, you know what the words: You do not know whether to laugh or cry means!

The further into the club you came, the more information you were told. At the meetings they were now discussing, people were being attacked or pressured. Which companies would enter the organization or, more accurately, what companies would be bought up. If there were very drastic measures against a person or company, we were very careful with such information, as the clubhouse and all other communications were intercepted by the police around the clock. The most sensitive information was then written on a griffel board with chalk. So, no one could clue what actions would be taken. Most often, only the police heard what intercepted us, like where we were going to go with the bikes or the like. It has to be extremely frustrating when they knew that we always planned something shameful according to the law. And so destructively, my life continued for many years!

Chapter 35

I once again went to a shorter prison sentence a turn that would be the turn of my destructive life. I got this penalty because of an unlawful threat. When they released me, I come into contact with two very odd police types that I have never met before.

Their first action was to send a policeman to the release itself. I almost got rid of it. A bastard who wants to talk to me when I go to my friends. John and Kenna are waiting for me and now it's a mess instead. Yuk! What is this for a trap, I thought.

Do they want to lock me in again? I had 100 thoughts in my head and not one single was of the positive variety directly. The policeman just wanted me to give him a quarter to explain, so I could do what I wanted to late or agree with his proposal. What is this? Hidden camera or? Did I wonder to the policeman? I understand you think this seems strange, as we do not usually do this, the policeman said! Yes, it's damn weird, I answered the policeman! I tried to think clearly, but if you have locked up, you're not so wide in your thoughts just when you're released! And that police knew very well about that. He tells that the County Criminal Intelligence Department had started a project in which they would remove those heavily organized criminals. I laughed at the police straight in the face, then it was easy as a clean sketch. What do you want from me? Did I ask the policeman? I want you to be part of this project so, we can run the operation itself. The project is based on the willingness of four heavy criminals, to initiate this to get a new life! Outside the criminal life, you kidding me? Did I wonder? No! Absolutely not answered the policeman! You're sorry! But to me it sounds like it's a dog buried! And the whole thing seems foamy, from start to finish I told the policeman. I have never ever heard of such operations in this country. Had we been to the United States, I had not questioned this operation. But in this country where everything is either Black or White, the whole layout feels freaking out! I understand your thoughts answered the policeman. This policeman thought it was a strange operation at first! However, pointed out and assured that this operation was anchored to the chief executives within the intelligence department. The policeman would take me to a motel during the weekend until the gray police came back on Monday. It was Friday! That was the day I had longed for it when I could meet my children again. But now I once again faced a life-making decision. The kids, the kids! What would I say for the reason I did not come and retrieve them? And I did not know for sure that this operation was serious. That the state would allow the police intelligence department to remove people and give them a new life. I think now that I write these words that it sounds like a movie and that this should have been a movie seen. But this is the gloomy truth about how it happened, scary enough. I told the policeman that I wanted to know significantly more before I decided. A decision that this policeman understood. The policeman took me to a motel named F1. The motel chain is F1 and you who have slept in one of their rooms know how small these are. It felt like moving from one cell to another. The only difference was that the windows could open if you wanted to. And that you could go whenever you wanted to. At these motels you only pay with a credit card and a card will be issued which was the key to the room you paid for. The policeman would I stay at the motel over the weekend. They pay everything! I received a phone number for this policeman that I could use this weekend if there was anything I needed or wondered about. It became a sleepless night! There the thoughts were very confusing. What did I do? John and Kenna, what would they think? But the biggest question was how my children thought! Were they sad or afraid that something had happened to their dad. I felt terribly bad and with a head felt like it would explode.

It was a weekend at a motel in the frustration sign spoken mildly. I did not have to call my children, as it could pose a big risk. I leave a powerful organization. An organization that had a large network of contacts. I knew how it happened when someone tried to leave the organization. But also the methods used. Tracking equipment and contact with different telephone companies had an entire organization an entire set of. Where employees checked phone numbers and positions where a particular phone was located geographically. Finding people was no big problem. But I had this information and broke the potential of all possible communications.

The weekend was really going through. I was very worried about what might happen if the organization thought I'd gone underground and started leaking information. I did not know what was waiting for me after the weekend when the policymakers who were in charge would come into contact with me. I wondered clearly what their claim to me was. Because they would claim me was quite given. The state should not let heavily criminal persons without supervision and give us new identities. This was just too good to be true.

I had heard about witnessprotection earlier, but then the person in question would testify to crime to get this protection from the state. I was very clear at that point. I do not wave a bastard, they can go to hell immediately. These thoughts were probably the only thing I was sure about. Becoming a golbag was something they could forget immediately, if it were their vision to be able to put some people there by giving some freedom and a new life. Then they had made the wrong choices. While I was extremely skeptical, I was also curious and expectant of this opportunity. An opportunity where I did not know what the price tag would end.

Early on monday morning around eight! Calling the policeman who booked me in this motel room and informs me that I will go to the police station in Malmö! Are you not really wise? Should I go to a police station? What? Calm down, say the policeman! There comes a police officer and meets you at the entrance. So, you have totally closed the brain function in your mind? I have never volunteered at a police station and will not do it now either. Which became my response to the policeman! The policeman thought I would be a little compassionate as they tried to give me a new life. That the state would give me a new life! Started with the risk of my life instead, when they wanted me to go to the police station. When the club was off with me, they started to search, and if they saw me entering a police station, they did not give them any good signals. The whole operation started to feel really wrong, and filled with great risk taking, for my own life. In my hand, I knew that the police department leaked information. That was nothing new! I decided that the club would check with its police contacts. I could only hope that those policymakers who were responsible could do their job and did not belong to the police department that leaked. I do not know how to explain how I felt. To suddenly just get taken picked and then lay his own life in the hands of a few policemen felt all but safe. Police and authorities, I hated so long, I would now trust.

Believe me when I say that the feeling was totally indescribable and scary.

It felt like I was standing at a big mountain jump and the risk of rolling down increased for every minute. At the same time, I could only ask a quiet prayer that this government attempt would really work. My friends were probably pretty clear that I would not come back and had prepared this move. They had a weak link. And weak links get rid of immediately.

Now it was a matter of delayed recovery from this fatal mission. I went out of the motel to go to the police station in Malmö. I had just received instructions that I would enter the reception entrance at the police station. There would be policemen who would meet me. They had many photos of me that they had over the years. I just step in and immediately a pretty tall and stiff person comes to me. He had a pretty Mc-guy like look, and it did I became straightforward immediately when I wondered if it was a torpedo or someone from the club's collection department who was awkward waiting for me to come. It was long-term, but not impossible!

It turned out that it was an intelligence police who, in most cases, infiltrated Mc Gang. Thereof the profile! He immediately showed up a police ID so that I would know he was a police officer!

This policeman said hello! And some credentials. Then he immediately said that we were out of the police station. He walks to a door that would take us to the police car's garage to go from there, so I could be put in security. When we got into the car, he regretted that his colleague was so upset because he told me to go to the police station.

It was the first time I felt that the police were on the right track and with the right safety tip when dealing with such an organization.

This gray policeman did not want to say his name for security reasons at first, but explained that they had code names. He said I would call him Black! I could not help laughing a bit, as it all felt ridiculous and unreal. The reason for that was that their real name would I find out after a while! When they read of me and really saw that I wanted to start a new life. The thoughts that came up in my mind were that this project probably had fallen sometime earlier and maybe for that reason they would not say their real names right away.

The car journey was quite long. Around 4-5 miles we went. This Mr Black as he was called asking if I wanted something in the store before we arrived at the house, I would land in. No thanks! Or yes! buy snuff! What kind did the policeman ask? General! I replied! I can buy some bottles of whiskey if you want it! This policeman seemed to know my need for whiskey, and it felt strange. But at the same time, it felt like they really had control of who they were taken away! And what it meant. Meanwhile, as Black was in the store, my thoughts begin to come up with my head. Police identification may be fake? No! Then the pass card had not worked into their garage. No, it can not be, I thought! Or? Mr Black, comes out of the store with a number of food bags he had bought, because I would have it at the place where I would stay for a while. We'll start the journey towards this place again. Now we were on a foamy forest road, or really crooked and foamy road. Probably not even on a map. As we drive on this crooked forest road for about five minutes,

Mr Black stops the car. Before he leaves, he says he will pick up a key and ask me to stay! Hm I thought! A backdrop where somebody's going to shoot the car with bullet holes! Even because he goes off, I thought! Now I was fighting at 110 percent and where the slightest sound or thing that was moving was perceived as deadly threat! Now you may think I exaggerated the threat image. But then one has to think about the life I lived and there, violence and other misery was my everyday life. In a Smith world, it may be difficult to get into the feeling. But to me it was incredibly excited and unpleasant. Mr Black comes out of the house where he retrieved the key. Then we go again, he just said! How far into this forest are we really! I ask?

We're just going uphill and we're late. We pass a garden with horses, and when we reach the back there is a large house of about 150-200 sqm. Where do you live now said Black! A whole house for myself! I thought! We take the food boxes and enter the house. A really nice house indeed! With open fireplace, big kitchen! The furniture was outdated, but fits well with the style of the house. It was a house with the upper floor and there was everything you could possibly need. Such houses have the police and those houses called Safehouse.

It's a house where they can protect murderers or people who may be in danger of being found. I ask Black about how many people knew this house? It just me and my colleague! What then my colleague ask I? I have a partner that I want you to meet! No way, I said straight away! Do not the whole damn police year come here and meet me well? No! But you decide if you want to meet him, but you can trust him. With all due respect, I can not say I trust cries, you get it all understand! I replied!

Mr Black looks up at me, where we sat at the kitchen

table and said! No! I understand that you do not feel confident and even less trust me! Then he asks if I thought it was so much easier for him to trust a Bandit? Hm! Undoubtedly he would have scored a point with that question! A question that was the beginning of some form of roleplay between a cop and a tough, where the rules of the game were based on mutual honesty and trust in the ground.

That I had a lot of interrogation with different cops was nothing unusual. But to start a trust structure, with a cop there was something completely different and new to me. What did I have for choice? It just seemed like the situation and see what time expelled. After we packed all the food, Black would go again.
I'm leaving you now, and coming back on Wednesday, said Black! What then leaves me? Why? What will happen now and, above all, how do we proceed? The questions were many from my side? Black says they want to give me a few days to land. To land he meant to get down my feet on earth again after all the fuss! Black went out into the car to pick up a bag that I did not know what it was for anything. When he entered, he had 8 videos that he thought I could spend time with. Then he said I could mess around, so I knew where all the things were. Type in the kitchen and the like! Then he said that we will see you on Wednesday. We said hi to each other! And then I sat in a house somewhere in Skåne in the middle of a forest.

The feeling I received was enough apathy, insecurity and loneliness. What happened? A few days ago, I was locked up and now I sat in a house that the police had arranged and where I received food from the state. The rent paid and with a very uncertain future.

Hope that you who read these lines shut your eyes and think the following, because I wish everyone can feel that feeling. Loneliness and you're sad, angry. You know that your children are in another part of Sweden and wonder if you as their dad are dead or alive. You should definitely not contact anyone. And after a long criminal life, their only friends are police, whom you hated for so many years. Where your whole life is now in their hands. It was like the frustration's knife breaks in my soul. I was depressed, so you could almost hear their children cry out for their dad and see how sad they were. Terrible, painful and unforgivable.

Now you should pass the time again! But I could go out into the woods on the walk and it's nice to just be able to do it. I doubt if I really made the right choice! Everything just felt more and more wrong and with such despair as I did to my own children. That I could only let everything be so damn wrong. It is totally unthinkable to me today. The first days of the house went quite fast, when everything was new, and the environment was also new to me. Where freedom was the destination. All new impressions made me very tired. Just fresh air made me very tired. Being locked and suddenly released took on the forces. It is fast becoming institutionally injured. One's body and mental state of mind were on passivity, and the guards ruled one day.
Just walking a little round in the woods and then back to the house to make dinner could create a fatigue that corresponds to a marathon. I had extremely bad fitness. But this fatigue was mostly due to my mental end. But I had my persistence left. It was, however, worn in pure laziness and well-developed comfort! I like everyone else, getting used to luxury. I had lived a very hard life. But far from a poor life.

Wednesday had come, and Mr Black would come around at eleven. Something Mr Black had called and already declared at eight o'clock in the morning. It was less appreciated that he called so early. When Mr Black came! Did he want us to go to a restaurant and have a lunch It was nice to go to a restaurant, I thought, then going out in the car and towards the restaurant. It became a small lunch restaurant! Pretty nice but small. The food menu was not directly impressive, but it turned out that they could cook there at least! I absolutely could not say that the food tastes bad. It was actually really good. When we sit there and eat and talk about how the police will arrange accommodation in another place in Sweden to me. Suddenly, Mr Black interrupts the conversation topic, saying that he has to make a call. He takes up his cellphone and dials a number. When the person Mr Black called, respond! Does he argue to say his true first and last name. He quickly looks up at me, with a look that said! Did you hear my name? I just raised my eyebrows as a confirmation, that I heard his name. Mr Black continues his conversation, knowing that I knew his real name now more. After he finished his conversation, he said that was his, boss he spoke to. I have only now after these years that his boss probably had a pretty good pressure on Mr Black! Considering that this operation was paid with taxmoney. We continued our conversation!
Mr Black wondered if there was anything I needed or wanted to do? I want to meet my children I answered him! We'll be able to fix that he answered! When did I wonder then? We must first review a lot of paper that applies to your new identity, such as new names, new passports and other similar papers. So, of course, when we move on and install you in your new home and life!

Where it can be! Answered Mr Black! I began to understand that it would be a long journey, and where this policeman would get as much information from me as possible. It was at the point we did not agree at all. Black asks if I think more about meeting his colleague? Yes, I have answered him! But not directly in any positive way. Mr Black noticed that just that bit of introducing this colleague made me much more with drawn. I just thought! A clue to ...

We finished the lunch to go back to the house again. Once we had entered the house and once again sat at the kitchen table, Mr Black began to explain that this operation had a set budget. Which means we must be able to defend the costs every villain cost. I wondered directly if they expected me to tattle someone (put it) of my former friends? No! Answered Mr Black directly! So good I answered! And tell this policeman Mr Black! That if you expect me to tattle someone, we could immediately cancel this operation. For that possibility does not exist and will never do it either.

Mr Black explains that before this operation started, the prerequisites were discussed to enable them to successfully implement it. The intelligence department has extensive experience of heavy crime and organized crime.

Mr Black says that the entire operation is based on the selection of the selected persons, explaining what crimes they committed and also explaining how they went. But also, that the old villain should give in any weapons or other illegal belongings.

I ask Mr Black! If the villain leaves weapons and acknowledges crime, then what happens then? Will the person in question be charged for this then?

No, Mr Black said! We take our weapons to destruction and then nothing will happen again! How do I know that you not only say this and then I get a prosecutor in the hedge? Mr Black was a little annoyed by my questions. Questions that were important to me and which in the event of a misunderstanding could lead to prosecution against me. How do you want weapons to lead to you wondering Mr Black? Yes, maybe through you, I answered Mr Black.

Now Mr Black was almost pissed off that I did not believe what he was saying. And explain once again that this operation gives police insight into organized crime. You should not tell me more than you have done. You should not tell who you performed the crime with and all you submit will not be a criminal offense. Are you with me, asked Mr Black! I'm with you I answered! Can we move on wondering Mr Black? Absolutely I answered! You will have paper that you can fill in when you are yourself and who you will leave for me the next time we meet, Mr Black said! Okay i said These papers are for your new identity and a form is for the new passport you will receive. A lot of paper I said to Mr Black! He did not respond to it but continued to throw one form after the other, which eventually became a little high on the table. Yes, I have to do, I said a bit ironically! Yes, that's fine, he said, the time will not be that long when you're here. Hm! You may call an ironic answer, I thought!
Have you been thinking about meeting my partner yet? Wonder Mr Black? Yes, I have done that! If you agree, it is best, because according to the rules we would rather work two and two! What then? Can not you meet me? Did I wonder? No, according to the rules, when the villain can be messy and then we'll be two. But you're calm now more or? Wondered he. Yes, you notice that.

I stood up to put on a pitcher of coffee. I did not drink so much coffee this day, and I started to feel one easier headache, probably lack of coffee. But you could easily get a smaller migraine case of all of these forms, such as Mr Black, presented on the table. I sat down at the kitchen table again when I sat on the coffee. Then I told he, that I agreed to meet your colleague if you are doing good for him! Absolutely I'll Answer Mr Black! Good! Then we meet him this afternoon, he said! Okay! Did I answer him wondering if he would accompany the house? Yes, it's so thoughtful! Are there any problems with that? Wonder Mr Black! No, I just wanted to know, I answered him.

We are going to go to Malmö Police Station today and take some new photos, "said Mr Black! What then? If you do not have photos of me, that's enough, I answered him, No! We need other photos on you. Not those in the criminal record, he said, and laugh for a second. That this Mr Black laughed belonged to the unusualities. I did not think he has that registry alike. In order to briefly describe this Mr Black! Can you say that he is probably the person on earth who gave the butteriness and control a deeper impression on humanity.

Now in retrospect, I can only say that safer cop one must look for. He really can do his job. The fact that he is today the head of the intelligence department is not surprising. So there, the police department has found a policeman who knows what word security means and where he really gets to do what he can. Just hope he educates more according to his approach. But back to the event ... We had begun going to the police station for photography, photos that would be my new identity. It felt extremely strange that you would be another person and where people suddenly would call me a completely different name! It felt like a bad spy movie, where the agent who saved me would delete my existence and now give me a

new name. I would be a new person. Honestly, it was a very weird feeling that began to creep at the back of my spine. Felt a bit like rubbing to a little, without knowing why. A cold feeling, perhaps more, was an easier form of anxiety. The fear that one's personality would be removed and occur in another form. Pure paper, but the feeling felt uncomfortable anyway. There were many thoughts and feelings that passed the road to the police station. I began to
realize that my life was extremely threatened and drastic action was required to allow me to continue to exist.

Everything that Mr Black planned was extremely carefully reviewed a number of times before he decided to implement it. When you only do things that are so planned, life becomes strange and you see life in a completely different way. I had lived a very controlled life. But a controlled life! As you do not control yourself, it becomes strange and tense. When we got into the police garage, Mr Black still had complete control. He did not trust all the police, it was clear. It's nice to me that I'm not just suspicious of policemen, I thought! But it was, after all, Mr Black's colleagues.

Chapter 36

Clearly you get confused when no police trust their own colleagues and above all it was a weird feeling when you're in the police's garage and Mr Black does not think we're safe.

We were going to the intelligence department and taking the photographs and it felt like it would be less tense to rob the Riksbank. I did not know why Mr Black was so strict in the polish house itself. But as I said! He was not of the chat-type.

Of course, he wanted us to take the stairs instead of the lift, thus reducing the risk of running so many Mr Blacks colleagues.

Right up at the intelligence department we would go straight to their photographer. There was a lot of cops inside their offices. They look at me and I who hated. One could easily get cop allergy.

When we entered the room where the photographs were taken, another policeman stood there. A narrow and almost flannel police. He barely said hello! He just shrugged his head and it was the way he greeted him. I felt anything but welcome to this, secret police department. Standing in the intelligence department was nothing fun. But there was inside the gray police headquarters. Police you do not want to do with. These cops were those who infiltrated Mc organizations and who had both equipment and knowledge to bug a fly if they wanted to. You were all so crazy. It felt throughout the corridor that someone was unwelcome. Not even Black stopped at any of his colleagues to chat or maybe just say hello! No, that was a very strange and unpleasant feeling.

Photographer did his job in 10 minutes and then it was out of the polishus again. I felt strange feelings all the time. I had been a criminal for so many years. And the last thing I thought was that I would be in the headquarters of the worst cops. Many may think that Säpo is the secretest in the police and security. But that's wrong!

These policemen were only six in all of Sweden. There were two in Malmö, two in Gothenburg and two in Stockholm. Then once again you had trampled into a new hell. But this time on the right side of the law. Probably what scared me the most. A page about the law I left a long time ago. But as I was facing again. Yes, it went well said Mr Black! With a determined voice and with peeling and scrutinizing look at the environment around the car we were in. Mr Black said it's supposed to meet my colleague if it's okay for you? Yes, I have no bigger choice or? Did I wonder more? Yes, we can blow it off if you wish. But as I said! We will work two and two. Yes, but then there is not much more to say I said! Okay! then we're going to drive said Mr Black!

Now there were a couple of miles in this car again. My brain went almost hot on all the issues that came up in my head. I thought that their entire department was full of foam. There nobody spoke to each other. I asked Mr Black what authority supervised their intelligence department?

There are Internal Investigators in the Police and there are some others like JK (Justice Chancellor) if it goes so far! What do you mean?! Going so far? It is very difficult to get our department reviewed for security reasons. And should it be reviewed, there is a lot to prove that someone has done a serious misconduct or the like said Mr Black!

We have the usual police register and our department has a separate register that only our staff at our department have access to. But crimes for which you have been punished will disappear after 3-5 years! Is not that what I said? Yes, you disappear from the usual police register, but not from our intelligence register, he said!
What do you talk too badly? That's when you moved in the circles you made. Then this is your price. Where you will always be in the rolls, Mr Black said, showing one of his few laughs with a lot of irony and sarcasm. I was terribly surprised that it just had to go to that. Felt like their entire department was outside for all outside government control. This discussion had lasted well, and we were soon at the meeting where I was going for the first time meet his colleague. I just had to ask Mr Black about their check on me because I was in the police's ASP registry (Police Capture Register)? He got a facial expression that a very surprised person gets! ASP said Mr Black, how do you feel about it? Have you missed the last charge I said! Mr Black said there is nothing about the Asp Registry? Yes, i said Have you really missed it? And I just had to laugh a bit legitimate against this control freak to crash.
Damn idiot to prosecutors exclaimed Mr Black! That you are entered into the ASP registry, you would not have any knowledge about. It's one of the police's secretest records,

said he very frustrated.

A statement that became the last thing that was said in that car before we arrived at Mr Black's colleague. He broke the silence by saying! There my colleague comes walking. Further on the road, a man went in a thicker autumn jacket and with a pair of dark pants. He had some self-locked hair and glasses. A pair of glasses that imbedded immediately when he sat in the car. Mr Black's colleague just turns to the back seat quickly and says Hallo kid! But he did not say his name! I ask clearly immediately after his name. Mr Black immediately adds a comment that we may get a suitable name on my colleague. I thought I could!

We decided to go for lunch and the restaurant that Mr Black had in mind was obviously several miles from the place we were at. The journey towards this lunch restaurant started immediately. Nobody was immediately talked about, which made the trip extra long. But after half a mile, this colleague wanted Mr Black to stay so he got a pee. When this colleague came back after relieving the pressure we went on. But we could only go for a few miles before this colleague again needed to ease the pressure. I asleep and ask if this colleague had problems with the prostate? You could think it said Mr Black! When this colleague got back into the car, I just had to say to these guys that I now solved the code name of Mr Black's colleague! He said I would like to hear that name. Given that your colleague must always relieve pressure and you call yourself Mr Black, I think your colleague can be called Mr Pink! But, given his pinking, it was a fitting name. Mr Black could almost stop the car as he laughed. His colleague might not be directly impressed with his difficulty in not laughing at him. A fitting nickname that still hounds him today.

Once upon a time at the lunch restaurant, it turned out that you had to eat how much you wanted for 65kr! Not because I had to pay. But I was a rather overweight person with quite a few kilons too much. So, in most cases, you were never measured at regular restaurants. This was indeed the happiness of a hungry Skåning. As we sat at the table, Mr Pink began to ask quite a few questions. He wanted to know everything! I did not want to talk to this cop that I just met it felt really wrong, what he noticed. But he did not stop asking for it. He was a funeral kind than Mr Black was.

But it turned out quite soon that these people would try to drive a classic on me. Because one of the police was unpleasant and the other kindly.
Then the evil and the good cop!
Clearly, I once again wondered if this would end like a flop where these policemen would try to make me a prostitute whore. Where everything was about to empty and forget.
So damn customer they can not just be I thought! It would be a thing if this had been common cops, who chased more and were not so used to it. But these policemen would symbolize this country's secret and gray police. They should be so smart they should be. After a long lunch! And with regards to many questions, we would now leave this restaurant to go to the house again.
Mr Black would ask me a few questions again ... Mr Pink would not accompany this time to the house. It was more the question that I would meet this colleague so he could join the house. Strangely felt everything! I could not let go of this Hollywood feeling and that just did not happen. But how much I bet in my lip, these cuddles put in front

of me anyway.

It was about time that I began to realize that I was taken away from the crime and all my friends. Suddenly I almost began to lose my foothold, purely mentally. Mentally, I began to understand and realized that I could no longer return to what I knew was safe for, me. My everyday life in the criminal world. It may sound strange and hard to understand for a normal person! But you get used to it and you rotate in the environment you live in. Although it is totally dangerous to the world, it felt safe for me.

But I could not say I knew that, though, I had two armed policemen in the way that would protect and pick me up. I'd rather say I was totally confused about everything that happened. Being able to get another normal person to understand the feeling of being removed from his everyday life and then being called for another name and protected identity on it.

I do not think there are so many words for those feelings I felt. That I could get new personal information and names may not sound so seriously. But only that moment is enough to break a psychologist for a quarter. Then, try to make sure that you as a person with these new personal data do not exist in the ordinary community. Should someone dial your social security number, there will only be a black page with information to a tax office and a contact person. But nothing about yourself as a person. To face such a hell, I do not wish my worst enemy! I can only say it felt like I was standing in front of a mirror and when you looked into the mirror there was no picture of my face there. An incredibly scary feeling that shook my whole soul. Thoughts on how my children would know if I lived or not were just some of those nasty and ice-cold feelings that creep under my skin. A fear that rolled under my skin and could not be touched.

I have done very stupid things during my active time as a criminal. But the feeling that I would live like a living Ghost almost scared my shit. Knowing what to come was, as if to look into his own future.

Mr Black continued his interrogation! Although he assured that these conversations were no interrogations, but only a survey of my own crimes. Yes! Dear child has many names! It was just so hard to once again review his crime career, perhaps this time this was a good purpose. But as I said it was tough, and very destructive to myself as a person. Since my crime list is not directly short. I repeatedly questioned these planning attempts by my own crimes. Since there would be no penalties, I thought it felt like throwing precious time in the lake. Mr Black said that this survey was the reason that the state paid my second chance in life. But because the state would bear the costs, they would receive a counter-performance from us four people who were involved in the operation itself. Since none of us four knew each other, I could not directly assess the carrying capacity of this operation. I would probably not be able to appreciate so much in the state I was in. I had not landed yet and it did not feel like my feet were even close to the ground at all. I tried to focus on Black's questions. But to sit and acknowledge crimes for a cry did not feel good. I wanted to trust him, but it was easier said than done. I was a mess, no matter how good he was at his intelligence job. He was very aware that he was very clear when, at the first conversation or interrogation, he vigorously indicated that he could not darken murder, drop or the like. So, I would have been guilty of such crimes I would definitely not tell. Because then he reports it immediately, when he is a, police like him so, beautiful said. Everything else he could swallow and dark, when these policemen were of the Gray variant. What I mean with a Gray cop! Is that these gray cops swallow almost everything, they are not looking to put your person. Without investigating only, the crime. Can sound like a moment 22. But then a gray cop works, while a common cop is black and white, and everything in between is a crime. But not for these gray police officers. Mr Black wondered where I had my weapons and other illegalities hidden? Hm! I have none, told I! In a naive and desperate attempt not to hand in my weapons. Yes, you do not have it, Mr Black smile a little and then said we'll take it later. Now it was a bit tight! Should I give up my tools. I think several times if this was a bluff and that they just tried to make me pick up the weapons so, they could go back to the detention with me again.

Imagine if that's the case? Crap! What my brain turns around. Could it be the cheatest intervention of the year to break down organized groups? And by lurking people's weapons they could bind us to crimes. Then lock us in again. Now it was like you were in an action roll where you suddenly became the protagonist of a drama that you did not want to be in. What the hell, I think? Mr Black saw ice cold out! Can he be so fucking cold, so he's sitting here and discussing my new life. When he may just try to put me there? There was no good stomach feeling I received. I only had bad vibes and which in turn made the whole conversation locked. Mr Black thought we would take a leg stretcher and we can continue for a while. I was not the least interested in any more interrogations or his conversations. He noticed that my interest in these conversations was not high on my priority list. He tried with all the different topics to get me interested again. But it went into one ear and out through others. My interest was nonexistent.

I opened the front door to get some fresh air. All questions and statements, on the crimes I made, could suffocate one for less. Black went out into the garden. It was his turn to slip while the iron was hot. Now he tried to get my attention by talking to weapons. You're a weapon crazy person! Sad Black, he knew that I loved weapons of all kinds. Only there was a weapon, so glowing it in my eyes. I understood that this subject was just a way to get into the skin. But it was worth it, we talk about guns.

He wondered what I thought about the police's new service weapon. Their new service weapon was a lift compared with their old ones. Sig Sauer is a good weapon, I said. But not a favorite. What is your favorite weapon then? To me it's a Beretta 92F, Strange said Mr Black! I also like that weapon. Yes, we had something in common for once, I said!

Chapter 37

After a long conversation about different weapons, we went back in! Now, these tricky questions started again I thought! But now I actually surprised him by taking up his service weapon. He took out the magazine and made a mantle move to make sure there was no shot in the race. Then he handles his arms and says I can feel how I experience their service weapons. I took his arms at the same time asking him a little ironically why he took out the magazine? He just looked at me with a look that guaranteed to say! Do you think I'm crazy or? I said, of course, I check your service pistol, but throw here the magazine, I'll check it thoroughly. Calm and nice now! He said!

Now we take it easy and quiet. I can take the gun again. What then? Should I not test the weapon? No! He said with a more annoyed voice. Probably, he thought that this would end up badly if he did not take me his service weapon. I asked how it happened to my children and when I would meet them. We are planning your meeting with the children. We must only anchor it with our boss who approves this, as it is linked to some costs. We must secure the area before you can meet them. Then Anna must also approve that the children meet you. It is not risk free and Anna has the custody of the children, so the only thing that can put sticks in the wheel! Is if Anna refuses to leave the children. Well! Then we have enough problems with big P! How do you mean, then, wondered Mr Black? Yes, I have put my last potato with Anna! And she is kinda angry with me! I understand that he said!

But we'll get that problem when it comes. Hello i said It sounds like it was several months before I could meet my children. No! Not months, but weeks possibly he said! Weeks! What then weeks? Should I become some kind of wooded before you're done with me. It depends a lot on you he said! How can it hang on me? I'm just sitting here in a forest and can not move directly! Thus! The faster you talk about where your illegal guns exist, so we can pick them up. The faster you will meet your children and start your new life. Damn! It's pure extortion I said! You can not put an ultimatum that I have to leave my stuff before we can move on. Yes, I can! I got crazy about his answer, on my question! Certainly! I would not get any penalties, but it was a high level of extortion. How did I get in this position! A mess that pushes me, it's absurd for a fan! I thought. We can take the rest tomorrow he said, and then he asks if I had filled the paper heap that touched my new identity? Yes, I have answered him very annoyed. Well, I'll take them with you so, we'll get your new identity documents as soon as possible. I went after the pile of paper and handed them over to him. He looked a little quick on the paper and then said it looked good. But you can say that industry and laugh in an annoying way. Black leaves the house to go home to his family! Yes, if you could only do that, I thought I was giving up!

I was thrilled to watch movies from the 70-80s. Mr Black had not rented the newest movies but had taken old movies. They were probably cheaper to rent! I thought it was very hard to sit there in that house in the middle of a forest. At all times, you were at ease. I saw things that ran out of the forest all the time or sounds that made me completely clear in a few seconds. To then return to relaxed, when it was determined that it was just me who was cheeky.

Having lived such a heavy criminal life makes it easy to become paranoid for less. I simply did not dare when I heard shady sounds or saw something strange. Could just be a shadow from a branch. That I respond to such little things can be hard to understand! But again! Chances could mean that I put my life at risk. So, on that front was my motto: *Trust is good - Control is better!*

Much of my energy was used for thought activities. For example, how tomorrow would be. When I'd have to sit with two gray cops and their destructive and boring questions. This roleplay as I experienced the police's questions like. Went on gaining trust in each other. I thought this trust structure was like trying to go on water! For so bad and hard, it felt. To trust these policemen. Yes! What to say! It was a difficult thing to do and that you had no choice! Did not matter better!

Early the next morning, Mr Black and Mr Pink came, I could see them from the kitchen window! They stayed in the car for a little while. They would put up a strategy on how they would leave me away from my tasks. Mr Pink! Be the first to the front door and with a happy voice he shouts Hello! Then Mr Black came! With its gloomy and controlled attitude. He said hello! But not so noticeably directly! Mr Black, the man who gave the control a face! Then, from the beginning, say Mr Pink, do not you talk with each other, did I wonder? Yes, but I want to hear from you, said Mr Pink. After telling me what I was doing, Mr Pink wanted me to sketch a place where I was in a hurry. What this purpose was for purpose, I can not understand today! Possible to record the crime in their secret rolls.

But otherwise I can not see the meaning of this exercise. We certainly sat for three hours with a crime. Certainly, we had our breaks when we went to eat. All these interrogations or discussions lasted for three weeks. Every day! For a weekend, I had to let these interrogations out. But that was not because I would have a rest! Outside that Mr Black had his family who needed some time with him. These policemen were very different in terms of the approach. Mr Black tried to break me with silence and isolation. Meanwhile Mr Pink was nice but could be cross-bound! I do not know how many times he said comments like that! If you do more crime throughout your life, I will personally pick you up for the slightest crime and put you behind the lock and boom for many years. Or he could say for a meal that he had oiled up the detention during the weekend and then he looked at me. An implied promise from his side. It was a bit of joke on the whole! But I take the message clearly! Mr Pink would not have hesitated the least! To pick me up if I had been guilty of crimes. Mr Black was the quiet type you never knew where you had, It was many times like talking to a wall. I think a wall is more outspoken than he is. These cops save my life! No doubt about it. At that point, I want to be extra clear. But we will return to it.

Therefore, I do not reveal their real names in the book. Their name stays with me until I get a ground with earth! After a lot of interrogation, you began to realize how extremely many stupid things you had done. But it was only now that we began to feel the consequences when these policemen were not late to point, out what pig had been, and where we saw the truth in the white eye. I find it strange that you can do different crimes and think they were cruel and smart. But now that you got it in your face you did not have so many apples high! It was only to realize that you were like a real maniac without taking in! But as you usually say! Late, the sinner will wake up ... Now it was as my psyche started to understand what damage I caused. I started to get very bad of all I've done before. But what did it help now? I once again had to try to control my psyche so that I could not get into the bottom when all the bad thoughts started. You can not hold it back for a long time. But I thought so! I! The very tough personality without feelings! Now faced with a new tough match with an opponent I've never met before! Myself!

To meet yourself is probably one of the toughest things a person can undergo! That's a real moment 22 Where you have to realize your crimes! Without bumping off your legs. Just like a boxer who goes into the ring and tries to floor himself, but not to do it, because then you can not get out of the match ring. Which in my case would mean that I could not be a regular citizen again but in order to be a regular citizen again, I had to address these heavy crimes I performed! In order to be able to re-enter the track of society again!
I began to understand that there would be a whole team of support people and others in the forensics that needed to be there! When I was to go back to society again.
I asked Mr Black how the package of measures themselves looked and what authorities were concerned. He responded that we contacted the social authorities where we have a contact person. That was good, I said! But what other authorities in addition to the police are involved. No one answered Mr Black anymore! But I asked for housing! Well, we'll get a close look, but you do

not need to think about it now. Everything felt clean to hell.

There was probably more chance to win on Bingolotto without buying the lottery! But this would end well! Now, something wrong, I said to Mr Black! What's wrong now? Did he wonder? Do not you like questions about where to stay and what help I will get! Belong to the more normal questions! You said he!
Here's what we ask, not you! Okay, I just thought this is going to be wrong. My mood went up and down like an ECG! I was angry! But at the same time worried about how it would go. I just had to succeed. I was on a dead end and you do not want to drive the head in the wall. What would my children do then? They already feel bad, by not knowing where their Dad was. And now I would not even get an answer to where I should live.
Could be Mr Black, I began to have a hatred against him. What he noticed! Then he put Mr Pink in place, so do not hear the questions and these hearings would lock! Mr Pink tried to raise the mood by saying that everything will be settled and that they obviously find a dwelling for me, they included them! Yes, it felt better when he said it! But the question was if it was just a strategy that I would not put into their questions. Mr Pink says that we would rather collect my irregularities in the afternoon or evening so we will not come. I wondered how this would happen? You are allowed to ride in the back seat!
I was completely mad! What do you mean or how should I be disguised? Did I wonder? We have clothes and other equipment And so it became!

With a lot of weird clothes and a longhaired wig we went to the places where I had hidden my stuff. We went a little later in the afternoon! It was a trip that took the whole evening. And a trip that went well! Although it was exciting that some of my old friends would appear. We went in two different cars! I traveled with Mr Black as a driver.

He noticed that I was on my guard. It felt strange to be naked (without weapons) but Mr Black said during the course of the journey to I did not have to doubt that he was protecting me! And he said he shot if he had to. This felt! Not sure for it! I had no weapon myself! And that I would only rely on this cop to shoot felt flawed!
When it started late tonight, Mr Black asks if they got everything right now and he wanted me to think carefully! Then I realized that there was a bag with my parents back then! It contained nothing that was legal. False securities! And other little and gone. But you may not need to get it. No! It does not seem so important said Mr Black! I thought so well!
We go back to the house again he said! Then he calls Mr Pink, who circles behind us, if it would be a gunfire with my old friends. He tells Mr Pink that he can drive home and that we go back to the house.
When we got back to the house, Mr Black would go straight. The time was around eleven in the evening. See you early tomorrow, Mr Black said, yes we do, I told you! Then just enter the house again, alone with a longing for my children that I had so bad conscience for. Then I did not immediately be this year's Dad, I tried to think one day at a time, because it would not be too hard and feel completely impossible. The hours went pretty fast, until the cops came again ... I was pretty tired so, I fell asleep almost once after I got to the house. But I was very worried. I was tired every day. That I could not sleep was not that strange. Who could sleep when faced with a whole new life, Not me anyway! I had to set the clock at

seven! When you did not know when they came. You almost never had a few times. Only if it was in the morning or afternoon.

I got up and made me order and drank coffee so that they could get a little spirited before they arrived. I never knew what they had in their planning. I wonder if even the researchers had the slightest idea? I hear a motor noise and look out! It was not the car I was waiting for! Now it was sharp! Just in a few seconds I was ready to go out and liquidate these intruders. It would soon prove that they changed their car for safety reasons. But I thought it was very bad that they did not inform me about it! Then the situation was tense without the need to make things wors.

Chapter 38

Once they had entered the house! Just tell Mr Pink that I would meet my kids today! What? Is it true? I wondered! Yes, that's what he answered! Why do not you tell me yesterday? We did not want to worry! Then you'd been awake all night and you need to be nice and observant when you meet your boys, he said!
Yes, that was a wise decision, but I was not mentally prepared for this! What was spinning thoughts in my head! What should I say and what should I wear? Lots of thoughts broke in my head! Mr Black says there will be a number of police officers in the background that keep those external security limits under surveillance. Me and Mr Pink will go in front of and behind you and the kids. Anna got up in my thoughts! She had agreed to this I thought, Incredible! I said loudly. What is incredibly said Mr Black? That Anna approved this. She does this for the children not for your sake, she wanted me to introduce to you!
I understand, I just said! Mr Black would pick up the children at Anna so he would only stay for a short while in the house. Mr Black says he has a bulletproof vest in my car, I will soon see you! Okay, I said concisely.
Now it started to, feel really unreal, should I meet my children with a bulletproof vest? How would my children take it? The kids would feel that their dad had something under the jacket I thought! What should I say then?
While I was thinking about what the kids would say, I

realized that I was, really bad otherwise, I would not need a protective vest, Oh Now it was, really hard.

That you should not be able to meet your own children without protective vests, Then, it's really bad I thought!

Mr Black went to pick up the children and to bring them to the place they had predetermined! Now only me and Mr Pink were left in the house. He wanted us too, go through the security routines they had. And he pointed out that it was very important that I did as they said when they were so called sharp mode! Absolutely I answered him. I would have had a protective vest. But then you were in the middle of any war zone. The fact that my brain linked together my guardians and my children was a whole new thing for me! I was very worried that my children would be afraid and did not want to meet their Daddy! I thought of what I would say to the children?! You wanted to say so much, but this situation was tense and military. Another concern was that their colleagues I had never met. And that would keep the external borders safe. Persons who would only be there for safety reasons.

It was not directly like going and picking up the children every other weekend, in peace and quiet. No! Peace, and calm, was the last thing, I felt before this meeting.
But I was so excited and had such a long yearning for my children, as I had not seen for a long time! It felt almost unreal, yes! My whole life felt unreal. Once we had reviewed their routines, it meant, in principle, that the whole meeting with the children could be canceled if there was the slightest indication that my old friends were in the area or if there were any of the other gangs that could pop up. There were many factors that recorded. But

I had extreme rules of conduct when it came to this meeting with the children. Mr Pink tried to cheer me up! By saying that he thought that would be fine and that of course they arranged another meeting if this would go

wrong. The worst thing could happen was if my children saw me and that we would have to cancel for safety reasons. The would be painfully purely emotional and that would make the children sadly idle! My children were certainly worried about them. But they did not know what was happening in the background. They only knew they would meet their dad. That this day would symbolize a day with my children was absolutely wonderful. But my whole body was in a state of emergency! I was prepared to protect my children, though I knew there were policemen to protect them. But like dad, you just think about protecting the children. I definitely did not try to reach my children if they blew off. Then we would just follow their safety routines and get back to the car. The children took them directly in security. That my old friends should go to my children was no risk. They were just looking for me! But I did not want my children to be exposed to see that their dad might be injured.
During the journey to the meeting place thoughts began to come up in my head! What was said at meetings in the clubhouse, everything that was written on the scoreboard was such information that we did not want the police to hear by interception. Things written, could be for example if a person we were looking for, had a safety guard or not! It could be of great importance when selecting the kind of ammunition that would be used. If the person did not have a protective vest and used armored ammunition, the bullet would only go straight through the person in question. And the person had a protective west and it used ordinary ammunition! Then the bullet would get caught in the

protective vests. All these thoughts are sour in my head! The question was if they knew I would meet my children or not? And if they had been informed of any corrupt cop?

Yes, it could be really bad! That they had the opportunity to pick me, I do not hesitate for a second. I had not revealed anyone, and it was good that there was no need for it. When I was sitting there thinking about what my old friends had for plans! If not, you became paranoid to the highest degree. I just thought! How can I act like a regular daddy with protective west and a lot of cops around me? How can I play with my children and hug the kids without having an eye on the surroundings? I got pretty cold when I thought about it!
Once on the spot, I began to become a nervous, I had a tense tension in my head that would not bring along. Mr Pink is watching my Protective vest as it should. Then we leave the car!

He dials Mr Black to check that nothing unforeseen had occurred. But it was cool! We were now outside Lund Cathedral. It was a very suitable place they chose, I thought! The place where I met the children was only 100 meters from this church. We started going so little to the place. My heart rate was at least 200 beat a minute! And my gaze flared over large areas. I wanted to secure the location myself, but also find out if it would be a problem. After a minute, I see my children further. They stood there with Mr Black, my heart was coming out of my body as it hit! I was happy, sad, worried, violent and with a pair of legs, which in principle moved forward by themselves. I just wanted to run to my children! But Mr Pink held me back for safety reasons. Stop saying Mr. Pink! What did I say! Ready to remove anything! Idiotic of him to just say stay without warning! Then he says that

Mr Black gave signs that we should wait. There were apparently personalities that were thought to be shameful and the outside team now check what types were. Maybe maybe 2-3 minutes! Felt like 2 hours and I was

not a person to go forward and say hi, To, now. What do we do I asked? Mr Pink, wait!, Take a cig! Have a cig? Who in hell could smoke a cig in this position?

So, we go again he said ... We started going forward again! Now the kids are watching me! And they want to run to me! But they are told by Mr Black to remain. When I arrived at my children! Then they became overjoyed and it overflows tears, I could not hold back my tears. The children were so happy they were sad with them. It was joyful years that were worth the word. I totally lost control when I could hug my children and feel their proximity. Just feeling their scent and their bodies pushed towards me made me almost completely shaky. Dad loves you! Dad loves you! I said how many times. My little son, Alexander, be so happy to see his daddy. A dad he thought, was more or less, dead when he could not contact me.
Dad, did not you think you lived daddy! And then he was sad again, dad where have you been? I thought you were dead! He could not say thought but said (Todde) I was about to break in. It hurt so much! I was the first time these cops saw, some kind of humanity, with me as they constantly perceived me as a gangster and a person without conscience and feelings. It's alright to show feelings, Mr Pink says. My big son Tobias was also sad, but he was more back wearing. He understood a little more! And that there was something wrong. Dad came with police and he knew I had no higher thoughts about

police.

He was really good to meet his daddy! But with some restraint. No wonder! This was not under normal conditions as we met. Because of going so fast I had not bought anything for the children. But both me and the children thought it was enough to meet.

My children had a lot of questions that they would answer. For example, I was living and those that belong to them normal questions!

Dad will go away for a while to make it better later in the future. So, we can meet as before. Can we meet you daddy wondered both of them? Later, Mr Black answered to help me with that question!

Chapter 39

We went to a cafè so my kids could have a soda and
cakes! Just seeing my children gave me hope for the
future. But the thought that I only had 2 hours to hang out
with my children before we had to leave each other again
was just crushing me emotionally. I did my utmost to not
think about it. It felt like just the time disappeared from
us. Soon the hour was over, and we had to leave each
other again. My kids were totally taken care of, daddy,
daddy! Where are you going? Do not leave us!
Pappaaaaa! I go under I thought! Whilst I had to give my
children hope for our common future and keep my own
peace!
I was completely matted! The kids wanted to have their
dad! And the question if I made them more ill by meeting
them, crawled at the back of my spine like a cold and icy
shine!

Mr Black tried to calm my children, something he
actually managed quite well! Mr Pink tried to take me
back to the car again, but I did not want to. I fought in the
other direction, against my children! Mr Pink understood
how emotionally this meeting was for us, which he
showed by telling me that this will be fine! And that I
have to give up my mind! I went to my children last time
and gave them a big hug and told them we will see you
again! But I could not say when. And that they would try
to stand out for it will be better! Tobias and Alexander
were so sad! So you can not even say it, even those

policemen were touched by it! Mr Black looked at me, he was wearing his sunglasses! I can guarantee that he even had torn eyes.

But due to his responsibility he could not let go and show a smoother side. He would keep alive and protect my children. I saw in Tobiah's eyes that he was worried about his daddy! But he has always been a little thinker. Alexander is the more spontaneous personality and immediately says what he thinks. Alexander did not think it was good for Dad to leave them like this. Tobias just said hi, daddy!
These lines are so hard to write! Though it has been so many years. My eyes get torn up immediately ... YUK!

Once the action!
That I should now be separated from my children was a fact! A very painful situation. But I had to leave the children. The police intelligence department was responsible for the costs and for all safety around me and the children. It was an expensive expense for the state to secure that place and that I had two hours with the kids, I would just be happy about.
Tobias and Alexander waved as long as we could only see each other and finally they were just gone. Felt so surely that we had been together for two hours, though it felt like twenty minutes maximum. Mr Black drove my boys back to Anna again and I went to the house again with Mr Pink!
I said nothing in the car! Mr Pink did not say anything either! He realized I did not want to talk right now. He said spontaneously! That even he thought it was terrible to see the children so sad. I just responded with a mumbling mm! We were back at the house and Mr Pink followed me to the door!

Chapter 40

I asked when this would end and when I could move on in my life? He replied that I will move over tomorrow! If my identity documents were ready. But he did not want me to be disappointed unless the trip was off in the morning. Everything was based on these identity documents. Okay! That sounds good, I answered him. He wanted me to pack less few belongings I had in the house if the trip was going to get rid of! So, I was done in case that!

I did not sleep at all that night. The kids were in my head and I had a cell phone. But I definitely did not have to call, as it could put me at risk. The frustration had got a new face for me. Not to call, though you could! I did not want to risk everything! Just because I would not be bothered by my frustration. Then I do not think the children would have felt so good because I called them the same day, we had to be separated from each other. No! It was just to suffer this hell! There were no other options I thought!

Mr Black called me around eight in the morning and said he's coming soon, but he also said that my actions were not ready yet. Okay i just said, then see you soon he said! Okay see you! When Mr Black entered the house half an hour later, I told him I do not intend to respond or participate in more interrogations or conversations. You do not need it! We are pleased he answered! It went much easier than I thought from the beginning! But he surely has a surprise back pocket. For such, he is like a person, I thought!

Well! What should we do now I wondered! Because he
had come to the house and we would not talk about my
crimes. I was going to talk to you about how to behave in
society and how important it is to not only kill people just
because they do not like you. But also, to keep you from
crime now more. You get a second chance in life and then
it's important to take care of it in a good way! Being a
Smith is not always that fun! And when the bills are to be
paid for you can hardly afford them.
Then you're a Smith, he said!

You can not beat down people and rob them or other
illegalities, hello! I get it more than I answered him.
Yes, I really think that you do! But we must tell you, so
we do our part in society! What you think is given is not
equally given to another criminal person.
You are four criminal people who are going to society
again and there is a need to adapt. In particular do not
violate the laws even if you are professionals in doing so.
How can you be sure that you have chosen the right
people and that we will be able to do it? I wondered? We
have discussed all individuals who are part of this
operation and analyzed your personalities and how you
have been doing. We can never be sure that it succeeds!
But you four had the best prerequisites of those people we
analyzed and examined, he said! But I would like to know
who will become my contacts when I've landed in my
new life? Exactly which these people are, if you find out
during the trip to the new place where you will live, he
answered!

272

I began to understand that something was wrong! Or it was very secret, because during these three weeks that I lived in this house, I always avoided these black questions. Why would not he be able to answer it? Could hardly be secret to me when I was the person who would be placed in society.

Meanwhile, as Mr Black was there that day, we went a long round in the woods and there I tried to the extent that I could not gather any new forces. I thought there were too many question marks in the whole situation and which I obviously did not know! Why? What's wrong? I went there thinking about this, but never arrived at any answer! Only more questions appeared! So, I released these thoughts and enjoyed nature instead.

The time began to approach lunch and it would have been good with some food I thought! Mr Black's phone rings, A short phone call! He says we are going today, your identity documents have come so we can go back to the house and carry your stuff in the car, so we'll later say he! Well! There smoke, that lunch! A Skåning's worst nightmare to get rid of a whole meal. We go to the Policeoffice in Malmö said Mr Black and retrieve your new identity documents! Okay, new life I thought! Felt like being a new person, with possibilities to get into society again I thought!

After an hour was now at the police station. He runs around and runs down under the police station into their garage. Where we three weeks earlier stood when I was to be removed. Stay in the car this is fast! Just get your actions. Okay! He leaves the car and goes through a sheet door. Here smells cops! There were a number of police cars while I was waiting. I was a little interested in what name I would get. There were three options on the form that I filled in and as Mr Black ago submitted to the authorities. After only 5 minutes he was back.

I looked when he got out of the sheet door. He had a white and large envelope.

He opens the door and says my new name! Terribly strange, it felt to be addressed by another name. I took the envelope with the police's log in one corner. I looked down the envelope and saw all identity documents! I picked up my passport to open and see what it was for a new dot you would be. Oh yes! Still, it was all in the picture but with new tasks in the passport. Feel like having picked up a piece of paper from a Cornflake package and found a new identity on another person.

Chapter 41

Then we drove he said! Okay, we do, I told you! With a little expectant voice. Mr. Pink will jump into the car when we get out of the garage and you can sit back and sleep if you want to say Mr Black!

We had a very long journey in front of us and I was completely finished as an artist of all that had happened in recent days. So, to sleep felt very natural for my part. How we took to my new home! Can I not reveal for security reasons. But it was a very long journey. When we arrived the next day at the place where I would start my new life! Come the first shock! They had not arranged any accommodation for me! But they would fix it during the day! I thought I would have a brain drain on these cops. I flew in the pit with Mr Black so he became really bullied and willing to let me down the road! Our grief subsided when Mr Pink thought we should see it from the bright side. And suggested that we go to the local newspaper that was available at the resort to see if there was any housing for rent. The police intelligence department paid the first rent then it was intended that the social authorities of the country in which we were located would be helpful with the remaining rents.

Everything seemed to suddenly hang loose in the air and I was so damn pissed on Mr Black! When he always said that it is important with control! Does he call that control? No, I thought so!

We arrived at a local newspaper! Mr Pink was in charge

of retrieving old newspapers for a whole week back. In order to find a home that they could rent.

We found a house after much searching. Now they wanted me to call and book this home. The old man who rented the house! Would only rent out half the house, which would have been so long! We could not get the same day but had to wait until the next day to look at the house. The owner was temporarily gone and did not come home from the next day!

Mr Black said, then it will be the hotel in the night that applies! Mr Pink agreed! I'm shit in what did I say, Is so disappointed in you! You promised that everything would be fixed, but that was not true! Then they admitted that they had promised it, but that their contact at home had gone out at the last moment. He dared not have an old villain in his house, I do not know? Anyway! So we should now go to the social authorities. When we got there we had to sit in a corridor and wait for the person who would be what I call my social secretary and who would pay my expenses. It was a her, this person became very nervous when we arrived! She knew there would be a man from a Mc gang and that the Swedish police intelligence department would come with me!
She started rolling back and forth with her office chair in the office. There was no doubt that she was worried! Mr Black said he's going out for so long! Now she first wanted to see a credential on Mr Pink so she could determine that he was this intelligence police as they were waiting for! He takes up his identification so it was settled. Then she would see some credentials on me! What's your name! My name is?!?!
I looked at Mr Pink so he had to say my new name. It

locked up! Then I was saying two names at the same, time!
How strange it became! As a conflict in my mind! Completely Suddenly it was just the new name that was about!

But my real name was in my spinal cord. The Social Secretary asked about the name that Mr Pink said sued? Yes, I answered her! Do you have any credentials that you can support? Yes, I have! And presented my new passport. Yes, there you're are, said Social Secretary who looked at the photo in the passport. Then you will receive social contributions she said! Yes, how much is social allowance, did I wonder? On your part! Then you will have about 3,400kr after everything is paid! In Swedish kronor counted.
I thought so! I usually go for a taxi for bigger sums every week, how will this go?
Yes, it will be fine, Mr Pink said! Sarcastic!
Yes, I answered him!
She entered my tasks in her computer, and then she said that now it's only me who can see you, since you have a protected identity. How good did i say Then she wanted to book a new time with me, so she could get into my situation a bit better! Then we were there. We left the social administration, to get into the larger city. Mr Black had already arranged a hotel room! Which we should now go to. I started to feel bad and felt what I was getting sick of! Which I also became! Really sick! Type stomach flu! Stay in a hotel and need to vomit a whole night! Be what it became, I was really dizzy, in my head and aching my stomach. All evening and night I would not even touch! I had high fever and felt completely done! Mr. Pink, coming into my hotel room at one time, You guys! Can

we look at these sketches again? I have some
supplementary questions that I would like to answer?

You, I'm not feeling right now! Well, then It's just
stomach flu you've had. Only I said, I'm completely over,
but I can see if it's fast, I answered him! It takes up to a
quarter, ok what do you want to know?

He started pointing at the sketches I designed in the
house! And asked a lot of questions. I answered those I
could! He seemed pleased, If, now such a cop can ever be
satisfied! After almost twenty minutes we were ready. He
asks if I wanted something to eat? I was just kidding him
saying the word food. No thanks! Okay, I fix some more
water! So, you get in your fluid, that's important he said!
What did you wonder about? Have you become human?
No, How, can you believe it! I'm just doing this for the
sake of the state! And then he laughs! I had to call him
crazy! He liked to hear that the wors villain perceived
these cops, the happier they became.
The evening went on the signs of the magpies! And I just
wished it would disappear. Next day around eleven
óclock Should we go to the house where I could possibly
live? When we arrived, it was a really big house. So, half
that house felt quite alright! Well inside this house! Did I
meet the owner! He did not seem to be wise in his head.
Confused Type! I was so tired of the flu, so I just could
not bother! I just wanted to lay down and sleep! Both
cops stood by my side! Yes! What do you think they
asked me? Yes, that's okay! Should you sign contract
wondered Mr Pink? Yes, I said, I looked at this confused
homeowner. Yes, it's okay, it said the house owner! Said
and done! I had my first home in my new life like Smith.
It was just moving in, when it was furnished and ready.

The furniture was included in the rent. I had received the rent from Mr. Pink before we entered the house! So, it was just paying the homeowner, for the first rent. Felt strange to pay his rent! I would have done as you would before. Nobody dared to get across if you did not pay the rent. But that was when I was Criminal! Now I was again a Smith!

The house owner leaves us in my new residence and Mr Pink and Mr Black, would go home again! I wondered what they thought I would do now? You should go to your social secretary at the time booked. Then you just do what she says! Is there any other contact person at your disposal during the first time? Did I wonder very much? There is one person at our department. But she's calling you! She will help you with things you find difficult. For example, government Mr Pink said! They do not like you! No, I do not! Mr Black tells me that I am now more like an ordinary Smith and you do not know anything about crime, and above all, you do not know about computers. Remember that! Absolutely I answered him! Very thoughtful, Hm! No computer skills I thought? These policemen are now leaving for home again! Yes, what's up with me now I thought? Talk about a quick course in Smith's life. This is not usually I thought, I was not so crazy, so I went to my new bed to sleep!

Afterword

Now you have read my life story and arrived at the end! You probably have many questions in your mind. What is your intention to have, because I personally think this is completely sick! That the state gave me a new life, I consider to be a modified truth. How did the state think when they left me here? I was not a Smith! I had a contact at the social office which was my link to the community! I am very disappointed in the state! Those policemen who put me here, just did their job. But the state that paid the call should have a safety net around us in a much better way. At the first phone call with these policemen who left me here, does it appear that one of us four people included in the operation itself! Had been executed. I was obviously no less paranoid of this message. But the police said it was his own fault when he continued his business in ancient Yugoslavia! To later come to Sweden in a coffin. The other person was injured. The third person I have no information about, and the fourth person is myself, I have not had a decent life today! After a few days in my new life, I contacted Swedish Criminal Care, where I asked for help? But I could not get any help without paper! We had no paper! What authority I even turned to, did I get the same answer! Where's your paper so we can help you! When I called the police again, they referred me to the female contact at the Intelligence Department. She in turn answered! That her task was just to help with forms or the like. Or if I wondered how to

behave at a date!
Yes, you read correctly! How I continued into the ordinary society! Or how did it go?

Made in the USA
Middletown, DE
25 February 2021